CW01315120

F.T. Weaver

Folk Tales from Ireland

West Agora Int
Timisoara 2024
WEST AGORA INT S.R.L.
All Rights Reserved
Copyright © WEST AGORA INT 2024

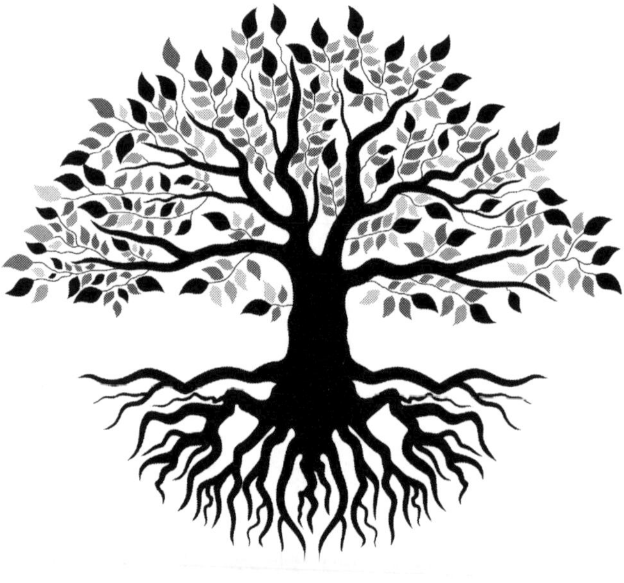

F.T. Weaver

Folk Tales from Ireland

Volume 1

Timeless Legends of Myth, Magic, and Heroic Tales from Irish Folklore and Mythology

Folk Tales from Ireland Copyright © 2024 West Agora Int

All rights reserved. No part of this book may be reproduced in any form or by any electronic or mechanical means, including information storage and retrieval systems, without written permission from the author, except in the case of a reviewer, who may quote brief passages embodied in critical articles or in a review.

This is a work of fiction. Names, characters, places, and incidents either are the product of the author's imagination or are used fictitiously, and any resemblance to actual persons, living or dead, events, or locales is entirely coincidental.

Published by West Agora Int
Edited by West Agora Int
Cover Art by West Agora Int

Discover a world where gods walk the earth, heroes are forged in battle, and love transcends time and fate.

"Folk Tales from Ireland: Timeless Legends of Myth, Magic, and Heroic Tales" invites you into the enchanting realm of ancient Ireland, where every story is woven with the threads of magic, mystery, and profound human emotion.

In these pages, you'll encounter the tragic beauty of Deirdre of the Sorrows, whose love defied the will of kings but could not escape the cruel hand of fate. You'll journey with Cú Chulainn, the greatest of Irish heroes, from his miraculous birth to his first legendary feats that earned him a place in history. Witness the incredible transformation and heartbreaking loss in the tale of The Children of Lir, where innocent lives are bound by a curse to the wild and lonely sea.

Unveil the mysteries of the Tuatha Dé Danann, the ancient gods and goddesses who shaped the very land of Ireland with their power and grace. Follow the mystical pursuit of wisdom in The Salmon of Knowledge, where young Fionn mac Cumhaill gains the insight that will one day make him a leader among men. Feel the pulse of ancient magic in The Battle of the Trees (Cad Goddeu), where nature itself rises up to fight in a clash of otherworldly forces. And be captivated by the enduring love and reincarnation of Étaín, whose beauty and spirit defy even the boundaries of life and death.

Each tale is more than a story—it's a doorway into the soul of Ireland, a land where every hill, river, and forest hums with the echoes of ancient legends. Let these tales transport you to a place where the lines between the human and the divine blur, and where every shadow and whisper holds a piece of the eternal.

Open this book, and let the magic of Ireland's timeless legends awaken your imagination. Whether you are a lover of mythology, a seeker of adventure, or simply someone who wishes to be transported to another world, these stories will stay with you long after you turn the last page.

Are you ready to step into the magic?

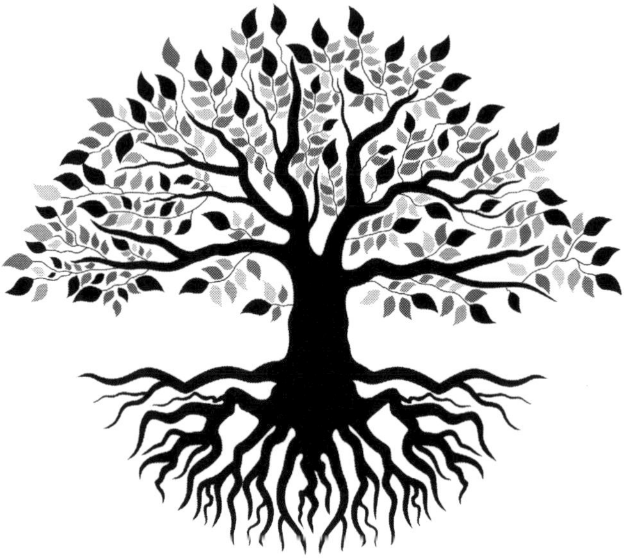

Dedication

To the storytellers of the past, whose voices still echo through the hills and valleys of Ireland, and to the dreamers of today, who keep the magic alive in every whispered word and imagined tale.
May these stories continue to inspire, captivate, and remind us all of the timeless power of myth and the enduring spirit of the Irish people.

With gratitude and admiration,
F.T. Weaver

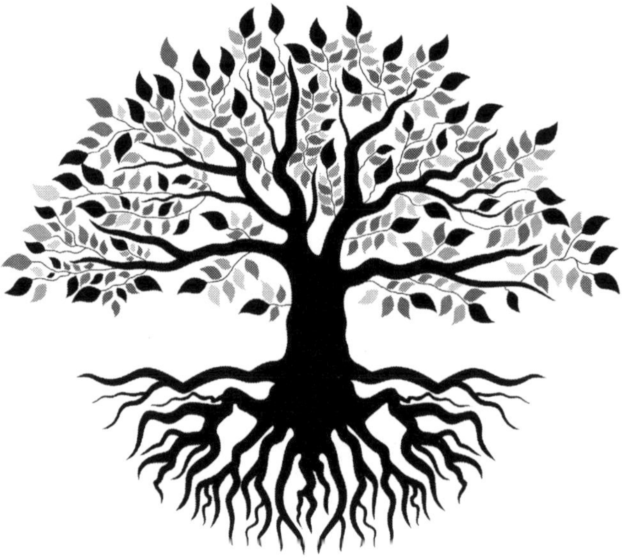

Table of Contents

The Tale of The Children of Lir 11

The Birth and Early Life of Cú Chulainn 26

The Tale of The Salmon of Knowledge 47

The Tale of The Tuatha Dé Danann 66

The Tale of Deirdre of the Sorrows 90

The Battle of the Trees (Cad Goddeu) 107

The Tale of The Wooing of Étaín 123

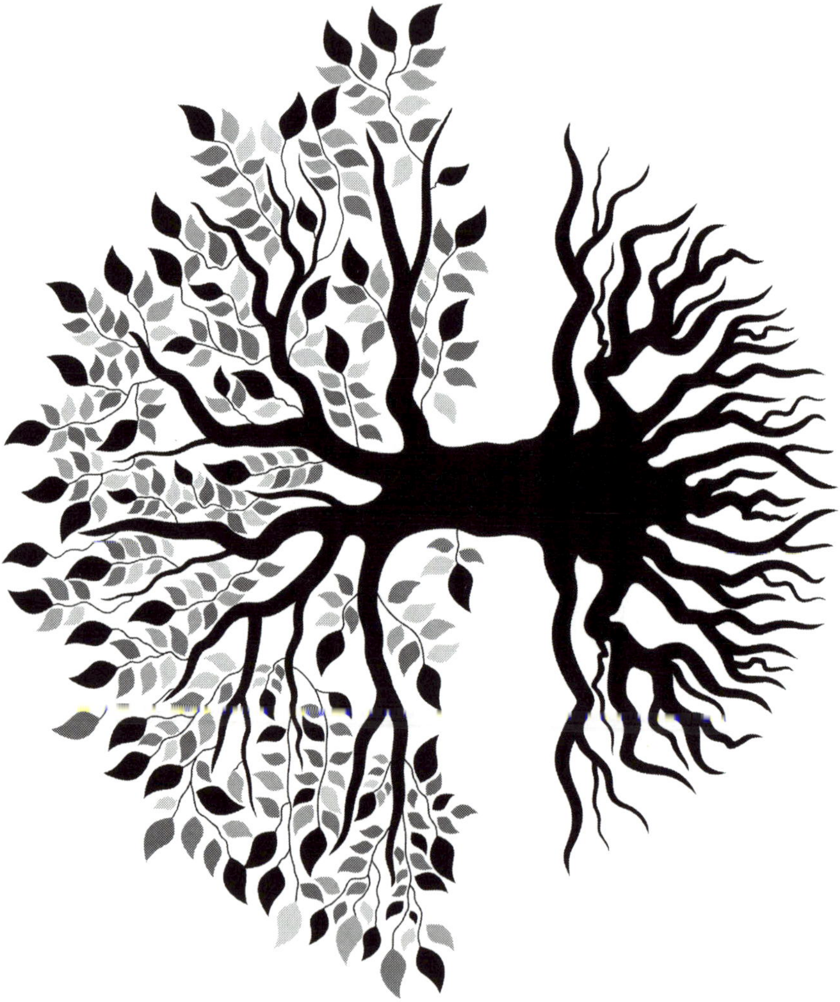

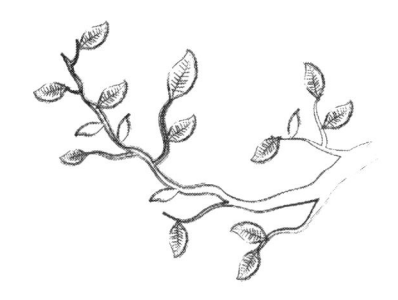

The Tale of The Children of Lir

Long ago in ancient Ireland, there lived a powerful and respected king named Lir, who ruled over the seas. Lir was one of the Tuatha Dé Danann, the mystical race of gods and goddesses who held dominion over the land before the arrival of the Milesians. His realm was vast, his wealth immense, and his warriors were unmatched. Yet, above all else, Lir cherished his family.

Lir was blessed with a beautiful wife named Aoibh, and together they had four children: Fionnuala, the eldest daughter, and her three younger brothers, Aodh, Fiachra, and Conn. These children were the pride and joy of their parents, known throughout the land for their beauty, grace, and gentle hearts. Fionnuala, with her wisdom beyond her years, often cared for her younger brothers as a second mother, and the bond between the siblings was strong and pure.

The family lived in peace and happiness at Lir's great fortress. The children spent their days playing in the meadows, learning the ways of their people, and listening to the stories of their ancestors. Their lives were idyllic, and they were loved by all who knew them.

F.T. Weaver

But happiness in this world is often fleeting, and the shadow of sorrow soon fell upon Lir's household. Aoibh, the beloved wife and mother, fell gravely ill and, despite all efforts to save her, she passed away, leaving Lir and the children heartbroken. The loss was a heavy blow, and Lir's grief was profound. He withdrew into himself, overcome by the sadness of losing his soulmate, and the children were left to mourn their mother in the silence of their home.

However, the sorrow in Lir's house did not go unnoticed by the Tuatha Dé Danann, and Bodb Derg, the new king of their people and a close friend to Lir, sought to bring peace back to the grieving family. To console Lir and to ensure the children would have a mother's care, Bodb Derg offered one of his own daughters, Aobh, in marriage to Lir. Lir, though still grieving, accepted this proposal, hoping that the new union would heal the wounds in his heart and provide his children with the love and care they needed.

Aobh was kind and gentle, and she treated Lir's children as her own. Under her care, the household began to regain some of its former joy. The children grew fond of their stepmother, and for a time, it seemed as though happiness might return to their lives. But fate had other plans, and the peace of Lir's home was destined to be shattered once more.

As time passed, the children of Lir grew even closer to their new mother, Aobh. She showered them with affection, and in her presence, they began to smile again, their laughter echoing through the halls of their father's great fortress. Lir, too, found some solace in Aobh's companionship, and slowly, the grief that had once gripped his heart began to ease.

Aobh had fulfilled her role as a loving mother, and the bond between her and the children deepened with each passing day. However, just as it seemed that the family might find lasting peace, tragedy struck once more. Aobh, like her sister before her, fell ill. The illness was swift and merciless, and despite the best efforts of the healers, she too passed away, leaving Lir and his children devastated once again.

The loss of a second mother weighed heavily on the children, and even the strong and wise Fionnuala found it difficult to comfort her younger brothers. Lir, overwhelmed by grief, feared that his children would be left alone without a mother's love to guide them. The thought of losing another beloved wife, and the despair of seeing his children suffer, drove Lir to seek solace once more from his friend, Bodb Derg.

Bodb Derg, understanding Lir's anguish, offered another of his daughters, Aobh's sister Aoife, to become Lir's new wife. Aoife was beautiful and regal, but unlike her sisters, she possessed a heart filled with ambition and jealousy. Though she agreed to marry Lir, her intentions were not born of love or compassion, but of a desire for power and status.

Aoife entered Lir's household, and though she appeared to be a kind and caring stepmother at first, her heart began to harbor dark thoughts. She soon noticed the deep love and affection that Lir held for his children, especially the special bond he shared with his daughter Fionnuala. This love stirred a fierce jealousy within Aoife, and she became consumed by the belief that the children were taking her rightful place in Lir's heart.

As days turned into weeks, and weeks into months, this jealousy festered in Aoife's heart like a poison. She could not bear the thought that Lir's affections were divided, and the sight of the children playing happily or receiving their father's tender care filled her with envy and bitterness. Her once fair and beautiful face grew cold, and her kindness turned to cruelty, though she hid these feelings beneath a mask of false affection.

F.T. Weaver

Unable to overcome the dark feelings consuming her, Aoife began to plot a way to rid herself of the children she saw as her rivals. Her thoughts turned to the ancient magic of the Tuatha Dé Danann, a power that could change the very nature of beings, and she began to weave a sinister plan that would forever alter the lives of Lir's beloved children.

As Aoife's jealousy deepened, her thoughts grew darker, and she became determined to eliminate the children of Lir. However, she knew that she could not simply harm them outright, for Lir would never forgive such an act, and the wrath of Bodb Derg and the other Tuatha Dé Danann would be swift and merciless. Instead, she decided to use her knowledge of ancient magic to exact her revenge in a more cunning and cruel way.

One day, Aoife suggested that she and the children should visit the land of their grandfather, Bodb Derg. The children, innocent and trusting, readily agreed, and they set off together in a grand chariot. As they traveled through the lush green landscapes of Ireland, the children's spirits were high, and they had no inkling of the dark fate that awaited them.

Aoife led the children to a secluded lake, known as Lough Derravaragh, a place far from any human settlement and surrounded by ancient trees that whispered the secrets of the land. As they approached the water's edge, Aoife's demeanor changed, and her eyes glinted with malevolence. The children, sensing something was amiss, grew uneasy, but before they could react, Aoife, with a voice cold as ice, began to chant an incantation in the old tongue of the Tuatha Dé Danann.

The air around them grew heavy with the weight of magic, and the once-gentle breeze turned into a howling wind. The children, struck with fear, tried to flee, but it was too late. With a final, cruel word, Aoife completed her spell, and the children of Lir were transformed before her eyes.

Where once stood the beautiful Fionnuala, Aodh, Fiachra, and Conn, now there were four majestic swans, their feathers white as snow and their eyes filled with a mixture of confusion and sorrow. The children, now trapped in the bodies of swans, cried out in anguish, their human voices lost but their hearts still filled with the pain of betrayal.

Aoife, though momentarily satisfied with her work, was not without a sense of dread at what she had done. The cries of the swans echoed through the trees, and for a brief moment, she felt the weight of her cruelty. But her jealousy was stronger than her guilt, and she commanded the swans to leave and wander the waters of the lake.

Yet, even in her malice, Aoife could not bring herself to completely abandon the children to their fate. She placed a cruel twist on her curse: the children would remain as swans for 900 years—300 years on Lough Derravaragh, 300 years on the Sea of Moyle, and 300 years on the waters of Inis Gluairé. Only when a king from the north married a queen from the south would the curse be lifted, and they could regain their human forms.

As the children-turned-swans swam mournfully on the cold waters of Lough Derravaragh, their hearts were heavy with sorrow. Fionnuala, ever the protector, tried to comfort her brothers, singing soft, sorrowful songs that filled the air with a haunting beauty. They soon realized that they could still speak and sing, though their voices now held a melancholy that echoed the sadness of their plight.

Back at Lir's fortress, when the children did not return, Lir grew anxious and set out to find them. When he arrived at Lough Derravaragh, the sight that met his eyes broke his heart: the four swans gliding silently on the lake, their graceful forms a tragic reminder of his lost children. The swans swam toward him, and in their sad, sweet voices, they revealed their true identities and the curse that had befallen them.

Lir, overwhelmed with grief and rage, confronted Aoife, demanding to know why she had committed such a heinous act. Aoife, unable to hide her guilt, confessed to her wickedness. As punishment, Lir called upon the powers of the Tuatha Dé Danann, who transformed Aoife into a demon of the air, doomed to wander the earth in misery for eternity, never to find rest.

Despite Lir's sorrow and his pleas to undo the curse, the children's fate was sealed. They would have to endure their time as swans, living out their long exile on the cold, lonely waters of Ireland. With a heavy heart, Lir bid them farewell, and the children began their long journey into the realms of legend.

The first part of the children's exile took place on Lough Derravaragh, where they spent 300 long years. Though their hearts ached with the memory of their former lives, they found some comfort in each other's company. Fionnuala, ever the protective sister, would wrap her wings around her brothers during the cold nights, singing to them with her sweet voice that carried the sorrow and beauty of their fate. The lake became their home, and while the seasons changed around them, the swans remained, bound by the curse.

During their time on Lough Derravaragh, the world outside their lake began to change. The old gods, the Tuatha Dé Danann, faded into the mists of legend as the Milesians, the ancestors of the Irish people, took their place. New kings and new gods ruled the land, and the ancient ways were slowly forgotten. But the swans, timeless and unchanging, continued to live out their exile, their tale carried only by the whispers of the wind and the songs of the bards.

As the end of their first 300 years approached, the children of Lir knew that their time on Lough Derravaragh was coming

Folk Tales from Ireland

to an end. With heavy hearts, they bid farewell to the lake that had been their home and set off for the Sea of Moyle, the second stage of their long journey.

The Sea of Moyle was a far harsher place than the gentle waters of Lough Derravaragh. Located between Ireland and Scotland, it was known for its fierce storms and icy waters. Here, the children faced their greatest hardships. The bitter cold of the sea pierced their feathers, and the violent waves tossed them about, testing their strength and resilience. Yet, through it all, they remained together, finding solace in each other's presence.

One of the most heartbreaking moments during their time on the Sea of Moyle occurred when a fierce storm separated the siblings. Fionnuala, fearing she had lost her brothers forever, braved the storm's fury, calling out their names into the howling winds. Her heart was filled with anguish, but her determination to reunite with her brothers gave her strength. After a long, harrowing search, she found them, huddled together on a small, jagged rock, shivering from the cold. The siblings, once again united, wept with relief and held each other close, vowing never to be separated again.

For 300 years, they endured the relentless challenges of the Sea of Moyle. They grew accustomed to the rhythm of the sea, the rise and fall of the tides, and the harsh winds that swept across the waters. Despite the hardships, they held on to the hope that one day their suffering would end and that they would be free from the curse that bound them.

Finally, after what seemed an eternity, their time on the Sea of Moyle came to an end. The next part of their journey took them to the waters of Inis Gluairé, an island off the western coast of Ireland. Here, the sea was calmer, and the climate more forgiving. The children, weary from their long exile, found some respite in these gentler waters, though their hearts still yearned for the day when they could return to their human forms.

During their time on Inis Gluairé, the world changed even more dramatically. The old pagan ways had faded almost entirely, replaced by the teachings of Christianity. The land was now filled with new churches and monasteries, and the sounds of bells and prayers filled the air. The swans, still bound by their curse, watched from afar as the world moved on without them.

As the final 300 years drew to a close, the children of Lir sensed that their long exile was nearing its end. Though their lives as swans had been filled with sorrow and hardship, they had remained true to each other, their bond unbroken by time or circumstance.

As the 900 years of their exile neared its end, the children of Lir felt a strange sense of anticipation. The prophecy had foretold that they would be freed when a king from the north married a queen from the south, and they could sense that the time was drawing near. Yet, after so many centuries, they wondered what kind of world awaited them and whether they would find peace after all they had endured.

One day, as they swam near the shores of Inis Gluairé, the swans heard the distant tolling of church bells. It was a sound unlike any they had ever heard before, and it drew them closer to the land. As they approached, they saw a small church, newly built, with a humble monastery nearby. A holy man, a monk named Caomhóg, stood on the shore, watching the swans with awe and reverence. He had heard the legends of the swans who sang with human voices and had longed to meet them.

The swans, drawn to the peaceful presence of Caomhóg, came ashore and sang to him the story of their lives—their transformation, their long years of suffering, and their hope for release. The monk, deeply moved by their tale, welcomed them into the protection of his monastery and cared for them with great kindness. He understood that the children of Lir were not mere birds but sacred beings who had suffered greatly and deserved compassion.

As they lived near the monastery, the swans found some measure of peace. Caomhóg often prayed for them, hoping that the end of their curse would soon come. And indeed, the prophecy was finally fulfilled. A king from the north, Lairgnen, married a queen from the south, Deoch, and the long-awaited moment of the children's release was at hand.

However, the ending of the curse came with a bittersweet twist. As the swans felt the transformation begin, they realized that their 900 years had taken their toll. When the magic lifted, the swans did not return to the vibrant youth they had once known, but instead, they transformed into frail, elderly humans, reflecting the true passage of time.

Fionnuala, Aodh, Fiachra, and Conn stood before Caomhóg, their swan feathers gone and their human forms restored, but their bodies weakened by the weight of centuries. Despite their frailty, there was a profound serenity in their hearts, for they had finally been freed from the curse that had bound them for so long.

Caomhóg, witnessing this miraculous transformation, gave them the rites of Christian baptism, ensuring that their souls would find peace in the afterlife. The children, now old and weary, knew their time on earth was short, but they were content, knowing that they would soon be reunited with their parents and ancestors in the afterlife.

As they lay down to rest for the final time, the children of Lir passed away peacefully, their souls ascending to the heavens where they would be free from all suffering and sorrow. Caomhóg, who had cared for them in their final days, buried them with great honor, marking their graves with a simple cross and spreading the story of their lives far and wide.

Cultural Significance and Context of "The Children of Lir"

"The Children of Lir" is one of the most poignant and enduring tales in Irish mythology, deeply ingrained in the cultural and literary heritage of Ireland. It belongs to the Mythological Cycle, one of the four major cycles of Irish mythology, which contains stories of the ancient gods and goddesses, and their interactions with the human world. The tale's themes of love, loss, transformation, and the passage of time resonate deeply with the Irish people, making it a significant part of the nation's cultural identity.

Cultural Significance

The story of "The Children of Lir" is often seen as a symbol of the enduring spirit of the Irish people. The children's transformation into swans and their long exile can be interpreted as a metaphor for the resilience and endurance of the Irish nation, which has faced centuries of hardship and oppression. The children's suffering and eventual release can be seen as a reflection of Ireland's own historical struggles and the hope for eventual peace and freedom.

The tale also embodies the deep connection between the Irish people and the natural world. In Irish culture, swans are revered creatures, often associated with beauty, purity, and the mystical otherworld. The transformation of the children into swans is significant, as it ties them to the land and waters of Ireland, symbolizing the bond between the people and their homeland.

The swans' long journey across the lakes and seas of Ireland also reflects the ancient belief in the spiritual significance of the land and its natural features.

Mythological Context

"The Children of Lir" is part of the Tuatha Dé Danann mythology, a set of stories about the divine race that ruled Ireland before the coming of the Milesians, the ancestors of the Irish people. The Tuatha Dé Danann were considered gods and goddesses, endowed with magical powers and deep wisdom. Lir, the father of the children, is associated with the sea and is often considered a god of the ocean. The tale situates the children within this divine lineage, making their story not just a personal tragedy but a cosmic one that touches on themes of divine justice, the interplay between the mortal and immortal realms, and the timelessness of certain human experiences.

Thematic Exploration

At its core, "The Children of Lir" is a story about the endurance of love and family bonds in the face of overwhelming adversity. The deep love that Lir has for his children, and the children's love for one another, is central to the story. This bond sustains them through centuries of suffering and isolation. The story also explores themes of jealousy and its destructive power, as seen in Aoife's transformation from a loving stepmother to a figure consumed by envy.

The tale also touches on the inevitability of change and the passage of time. The children's 900-year exile takes them from the age of the Tuatha Dé Danann into the era of Christianity in Ireland. This transition reflects the historical and cultural changes that Ireland underwent over the centuries, from its pagan roots to its Christian present. The children's transformation back into their human forms at the end of the tale, only to die shortly thereafter, symbolizes the inevitable end of an era and the transition to a new one.

Literary Influence

"The Children of Lir" has had a profound influence on Irish literature and arts. The story has been retold and adapted in numerous forms, including poetry, plays, and music. It has inspired countless Irish writers, from the ancient bards who first told the story to modern poets and playwrights. The tale's themes of transformation and exile have resonated with many Irish writers, particularly those writing during times of political and social upheaval, such as the Irish Literary Revival in the late 19th and early 20th centuries.

The story has also been a source of inspiration for visual artists. The image of the swans on the lonely lakes and seas of Ireland is a powerful and evocative symbol that has been depicted in paintings, sculptures, and stained glass. These representations often emphasize the beauty and melancholy of the tale, highlighting the deep emotional resonance that the story holds.

Connection to Irish National Identity

"The Children of Lir" is often seen as an allegory for the Irish experience, particularly in the context of the country's history of colonization and the struggle for independence. The children's transformation and exile can be interpreted as a metaphor for the displacement and suffering of the Irish people under foreign rule. Their eventual release and return to their human forms symbolize the hope for national liberation and the restoration of

Ireland's cultural identity.

During the Irish Literary Revival, which sought to reclaim and celebrate Ireland's rich cultural heritage, "The Children of Lir" was often invoked as a symbol of the enduring spirit of the Irish nation. The story was retold and adapted in ways that emphasized its relevance to contemporary struggles for cultural and political independence. It became a touchstone for writers and artists seeking to express a sense of national identity rooted in the ancient myths and legends of Ireland.

Religious and Spiritual Dimensions

The tale also has a significant religious and spiritual dimension, particularly in its later Christianized versions. The children's baptism by the monk Caomhóg and their peaceful death at the end of the story can be seen as a Christian redemption narrative, where the suffering endured by the innocent is ultimately rewarded with spiritual salvation. This Christian overlay on an originally pagan tale reflects the complex interplay between Ireland's pagan and Christian traditions.

The story also resonates with the Celtic belief in the soul's journey and the idea of transformation as a spiritual process. The children's transformation into swans can be seen as a form of soul exile, where they are cut off from their human existence and forced to live in a liminal state between worlds. Their eventual return to human form and death can be interpreted as a return to the natural order and a release from the cycle of suffering, aligning with the Celtic notion of the soul's journey through different states of being.

The Tale's Legacy in Modern Ireland

Today, "The Children of Lir" remains one of the most beloved and well-known Irish folktales. It is taught in schools, performed in theaters, and celebrated in festivals across Ireland. The story's themes of family, love, resilience, and the power of transformation continue to resonate with audiences of all ages.

The tale is also commemorated in various cultural and historical sites across Ireland. Lough Derravaragh, where the children spent the first part of their exile, is a place of pilgrimage for those who wish to connect with the story's deep cultural roots. Similarly, sites associated with the other parts of their journey, such as the Sea of Moyle, are celebrated in local folklore and tourism.

In modern popular culture, the story has been adapted into novels, films, and even children's books, ensuring that it continues to be passed down through generations. These modern retellings often explore the story's emotional depth and its relevance to contemporary issues, such as the importance of family and the experience of loss and redemption.

Conclusion

"The Children of Lir" is more than just a tale of mythological tragedy; it is a story that encapsulates the essence of Irish culture, with its deep connections to the land, its history of endurance in the face of adversity, and its rich spiritual traditions. The tale's enduring popularity speaks to its universal themes of love, loss, and the passage of time, which continue to resonate with people today. Whether seen as a metaphor for the Irish national experience, a reflection on the nature of transformation and exile, or a simple but powerful story of familial love, "The Children of Lir" remains a cornerstone of Ireland's cultural heritage, a story that speaks to the heart of what it means to be human.

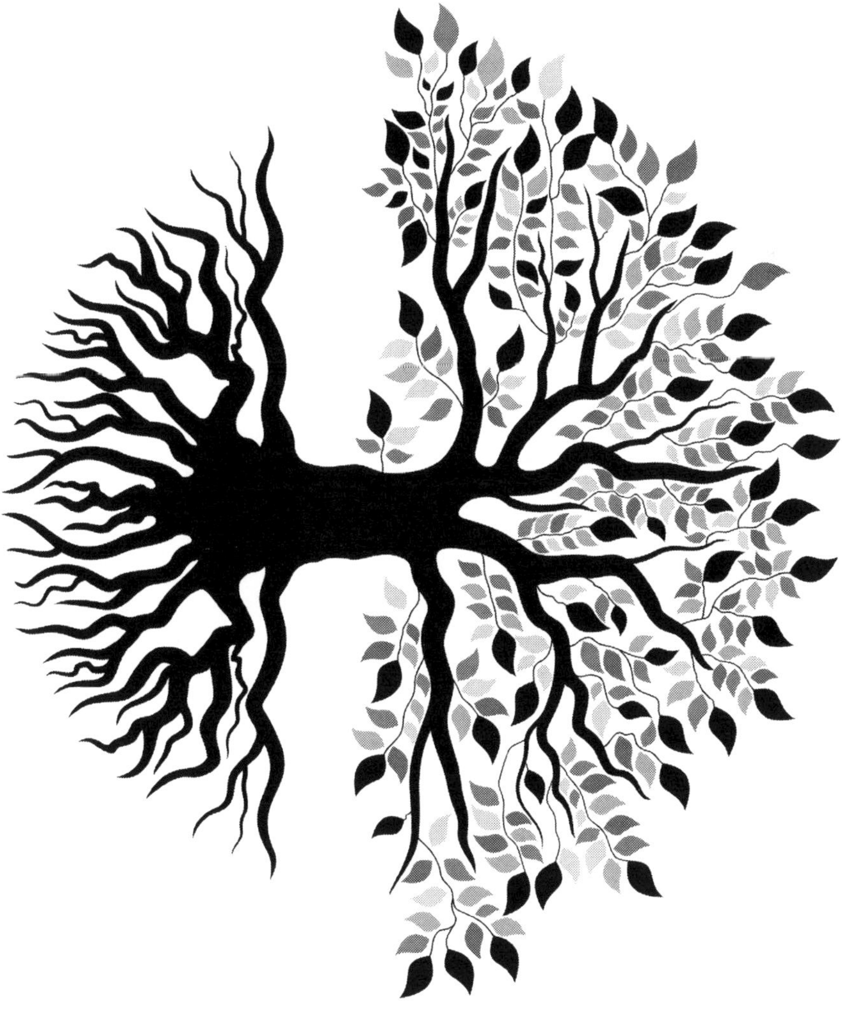

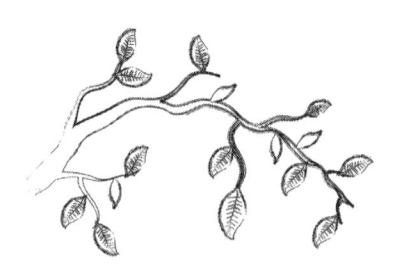

The Tale of The Birth and Early Life of Cú Chulainn

In the ancient kingdom of Ulster, long before the days of recorded history, a prophecy whispered through the halls of Emain Macha, the seat of King Conchobar mac Nessa. This prophecy spoke of a child who would be born with extraordinary strength and unparalleled courage, a hero who would defend Ulster in its darkest hour. This child would grow to become Cú Chulainn, the Hound of Ulster, one of the greatest warriors ever known.

The tale of Cú Chulainn's birth begins with his parents, Dechtire and Sualtam. Dechtire was the sister of King Conchobar and a woman of noble beauty and grace. One evening, as she dined with her brother and the nobles of Ulster, a strange and powerful event took place. A bright, otherworldly bird appeared in the hall, dazzling the court with its splendor. The bird led Dechtire and her handmaidens out of Emain Macha, and they followed it into the wilderness.

For three days and three nights, the women were lost to the world, until they were found sheltering in a grand house in the otherworldly realm of the Sidhe, the land of the fairies. There, they were cared for by a mysterious man of great stature and nobility, who revealed himself to be the god Lugh of the Long Arm, one of the most powerful deities of the Tuatha Dé Danann.

Lugh had chosen Dechtire to bear his child, a son who would inherit both the divine strength of the gods and the human courage of the Ulster warriors. Dechtire, unaware of the god's true nature at first, was captivated by him, and they were joined together. When she returned to Ulster, Dechtire carried within her the seed of this miraculous union.

Soon after her return, Dechtire realized she was pregnant, and the court of Ulster buzzed with excitement and curiosity about the child she would bear. However, Dechtire, fearing the potential wrath of her brother Conchobar or the implications of her mysterious pregnancy, tried to keep her condition secret for as long as possible. But the signs were undeniable, and when the time came, she gave birth to a beautiful and healthy baby boy.

The child was named Setanta, and from the moment of his birth, it was clear that he was no ordinary boy. He was strong and vigorous, with a spark in his eyes that spoke of his extraordinary lineage. The druids and wise men of Ulster prophesied great things for Setanta, predicting that he would grow to be a mighty warrior, a protector of the kingdom, and a hero whose fame would spread far beyond the shores of Ireland.

King Conchobar, recognizing the potential in his young nephew, took Setanta under his wing and ensured that he was raised with all the privileges and training befitting a future warrior. Setanta was taught by the best warriors, trained in the arts of combat, and educated in the ways of kings and heroes. Even as a young child, he demonstrated extraordinary abilities that set him apart from his peers.

But while Setanta's divine parentage and royal upbringing laid the foundation for his future, it was his own courage, determination, and indomitable spirit that would define his early years and the path he would take. From a tender age, he sought to prove himself, eager to match the deeds of the greatest heroes and warriors he heard about in the stories told around the fires of Emain Macha.

Setanta's journey toward becoming Cú Chulainn would begin not with a great battle or a grand adventure, but with a simple game—a boy's game of hurling that would soon turn into a test of life and death.

As Setanta grew, his extraordinary nature became even more evident. From a very young age, he displayed remarkable strength, agility, and a keen mind that belied his years. His peers, the other boys of Emain Macha, were both in awe of and intimidated by him. Setanta's desire to prove himself as a warrior was unyielding, and he sought every opportunity to demonstrate his prowess.

One day, when Setanta was still a child of only six years old, he heard that the king and his court were attending a feast at the house of the great smith, Culann. The feast was to be a grand affair, with music, games, and the telling of heroic tales, and it was set to take place after a day of sport and hunting. Setanta, though young, had already earned a reputation for his skill in hurling, the ancient game played with a ball and stick that demanded both strength and precision. He wished to join the king and the warriors at the feast, but he also longed to test his skills against the older boys in a hurling match.

As the day of the feast arrived, Setanta set out to join the boys' game, determined to prove himself. With his hurley stick and ball in hand, he played with such intensity that he outclassed every boy on the field. His strength, speed, and sheer willpower were unmatched, and it became clear to everyone that he was no ordinary child. Yet, so engrossed was he in the game that he lost track of time, and soon the king and his retinue had left for Culann's house without him.

Undeterred, Setanta decided to follow on his own. He would not miss the feast or the chance to be among the warriors of Ulster. He slung his hurley stick over his shoulder and set out across the fields, making his way toward Culann's forge. As the sun began to set, he arrived at the gates of Culann's house, unaware of the danger that awaited him.

Culann, not knowing that Setanta was on his way, had already asked King Conchobar if everyone had arrived. When the king confirmed that all his guests were present, Culann unleashed his ferocious guard dog to protect his home. This hound was no ordinary beast—it was a massive, fearsome creature, bred to protect the smith's property and trained to be utterly merciless to any intruder.

As Setanta approached, the hound caught his scent and bounded towards him with terrifying speed. The boy saw the beast charging at him, its fangs bared and its eyes glowing with the thrill of the hunt. But Setanta, young as he was, did not flinch. Instead, he stood his ground, his heart steady, his mind clear.

With the quick reflexes of a warrior born, Setanta seized his hurley stick and hurled his ball with all his might. The ball flew straight and true, striking the hound in its open mouth and lodging deep in its throat. The force of the blow was so great that it killed the hound instantly, and the massive beast collapsed at the boy's feet.

Hearing the commotion, the men of the court, along with King Conchobar and Culann, rushed outside to see what had happened. They were greeted by the sight of young Setanta standing triumphantly over the body of the dead hound. The warriors marveled at the boy's courage and skill, but their admiration was tinged with concern. Culann, in particular, was distraught, for the hound had been not only his guardian but also a cherished companion.

Realizing the gravity of what he had done, Setanta approached Culann with a solemn expression. Although he had acted in self-defense, he felt a deep sense of responsibility for the loss Culann had suffered. In a gesture that would mark him as a true hero, Setanta offered to take the place of the hound.

"I will guard your house in the hound's place," Setanta said to Culann, "until you can rear another that is as strong and as loyal as the one I have slain."

This offer astonished everyone present. It was a testament not only to Setanta's bravery but also to his sense of honor and duty. Culann, moved by the boy's sincerity, accepted the offer, though he assured Setanta that he would not be expected to live as a guard dog. Instead, the warriors and nobles present praised Setanta's courage and agreed that from that day forward, he would be known by a new name: Cú Chulainn, meaning "the Hound of Culann."

This event marked the beginning of Cú Chulainn's legendary career. His new name reflected his status as a warrior of extraordinary skill and his willingness to protect those in need, even at a young age. The tale of how he had slain the great hound and offered to take its place spread quickly throughout Ulster, and it became the first of many stories that would be told about him in the halls of Emain Macha and beyond.

Cú Chulainn's early exploits did not end with the slaying of the hound. As he grew older, his fame and prowess would only continue to increase, setting the stage for the many great deeds he would perform in the years to come.

After the slaying of the hound and the bestowal of his new name, Cú Chulainn's reputation began to spread throughout the land of Ulster. He was still a boy, but his deeds had already marked him as someone destined for greatness. Despite his youth, he was determined to prove himself worthy of the name he had been given and the expectations that came with it.

In Emain Macha, the royal seat of Ulster, young boys were trained to become warriors, learning the arts of combat, strategy, and leadership. This training was rigorous and demanding, designed to prepare them for the battles they would face as men. The boys who trained here were the future champions of Ulster, and among them were many who would go on to achieve fame in their own right. But none were quite like Cú Chulainn.

One day, Cú Chulainn decided to join the boys at their training, eager to measure his skills against theirs. He was younger than most of them, but his heart burned with the desire to prove his worth. As he approached the playing field where the boys were engaged in their martial exercises, he carried with him his hurley stick and ball, symbols of his prowess in the game of hurling, which was as much a test of strength and agility as it was a game.

When the other boys saw Cú Chulainn approaching, they were initially dismissive. After all, he was younger and smaller than most of them, and they did not believe he could compete at their level. But Cú Chulainn, undeterred by their skepticism, asked to join in their games.

The boys agreed, but with a hidden agenda: they planned to teach this young upstart a lesson. They allowed him to enter the game, intending to overwhelm him with their numbers and superior size. But Cú Chulainn was no ordinary boy, and they soon realized the mistake they had made.

F.T. Weaver

As the game began, Cú Chulainn's natural prowess quickly became evident. He darted across the field with a speed that none could match, his movements precise and fluid. He outmaneuvered his opponents with ease, scoring goal after goal. The other boys, realizing they were facing someone far beyond their skill level, grew frustrated and intensified their efforts to bring him down.

But the more they pushed, the more Cú Chulainn's talents shone. In the heat of the game, a transformation began to take place within him—a manifestation of his divine heritage and his warrior spirit. His face grew fierce, his muscles tensed with supernatural strength, and his eyes gleamed with a fiery intensity that sent shivers through the spines of those who dared to oppose him.

This transformation was known as the ríastrad, or the warp-spasm, a state of battle frenzy where Cú Chulainn's body contorted and his strength became unmatched. In this state, he was invincible, a whirlwind of fury and power that none could withstand. The boys, now terrified, realized they were no match for Cú Chulainn. They fled the field, leaving him victorious and alone.

King Conchobar, who had been observing the events from afar, was astonished by what he had seen. He recognized that Cú Chulainn was no ordinary child and that his potential as a warrior was limitless. Conchobar knew that Cú Chulainn's talents needed to be nurtured and honed if he were to fulfill his destiny as the champion of Ulster.

After the game, the king approached Cú Chulainn and praised him for his extraordinary skills. He invited Cú Chulainn to join the Red Branch Knights, the elite warriors of Ulster who were known for their bravery, strength, and loyalty. It was an incredible honor, one that was rarely bestowed upon someone so young, but Cú Chulainn had already proven that he was no ordinary boy.

Cú Chulainn accepted the offer with gratitude, eager to continue his training among the best warriors in the land. He knew that his journey had only just begun and that there were many challenges ahead. But he was determined to meet each one with the same courage and determination that had brought him this far.

Under the guidance of the Red Branch Knights, Cú Chulainn's training intensified. He learned the art of swordsmanship, the use of the spear, and the tactics of war. He studied under the greatest warriors of Ulster, absorbing their knowledge and refining his skills. But even among these seasoned warriors, Cú Chulainn stood out. His strength, speed, and agility were unparalleled, and his ability to enter the ríastrad made him nearly invincible in battle.

As he trained, Cú Chulainn also began to develop a sense of strategy and leadership. He understood that being a great warrior was not just about physical strength but also about intelligence, wisdom, and the ability to inspire others. He formed strong bonds with the other warriors, earning their respect and admiration.

One of Cú Chulainn's most remarkable traits was his unbreakable sense of honor. He upheld the warrior's code with unwavering integrity, always seeking to do what was right, even when it was difficult. This sense of honor would define his actions in the years to come, guiding him through the many trials and battles that lay ahead.

Cú Chulainn's early exploits did more than just establish his reputation—they foreshadowed the greatness that would come. His training with the boys of Emain Macha and the Red Branch Knights laid the foundation for his future as the greatest warrior in all of Ireland. But even as he trained, Cú Chulainn knew that he was destined for something more. His journey was far from over, and the challenges that awaited him would test his strength, courage, and honor like never before.

As Cú Chulainn continued his training and grew in strength and skill, word of his extraordinary abilities spread far and wide. He was no longer just the young Setanta who had killed a ferocious hound; he was now recognized as a warrior of immense potential, destined to become the greatest champion of Ulster. Yet, even with his growing fame, Cú Chulainn remained humble and eager to prove himself further.

One of the most significant tests of his early life came in the form of the Spancel Hoop, a legendary challenge that would cement his reputation as a fearless and resourceful warrior.

The challenge arose during a time of great tension between the warriors of Ulster and their rivals. A powerful and cunning warrior named Bricriu of the Bitter Tongue had long been known for his ability to sow discord and stir up trouble among the nobles of Ulster. Bricriu, always eager to cause mischief, devised a scheme to provoke the warriors into a contest of bravery and strength.

Bricriu constructed a grand feasting hall, inviting the greatest warriors of Ulster to a banquet. The hall was adorned with the finest decorations, and the feast was prepared with the most sumptuous foods. Bricriu promised that the evening would be a celebration of Ulster's might and glory. However, true to his nature, Bricriu had a hidden agenda.

During the feast, Bricriu presented the warriors with a challenge: whoever could take up the Spancel Hoop, a seemingly simple object but imbued with magical properties, and guard it through the night would be declared the greatest hero of Ulster. The Spancel Hoop was no ordinary hoop—it was a dangerous artifact, said to summon terrifying apparitions and monstrous foes that would test the courage of any man who dared to possess it.

The warriors, eager to prove their mettle, debated who among them was most worthy of the challenge. Each boasted of their past deeds and strength, and tensions began to rise. Bricriu, delighted by the discord he had sown, watched as the warriors argued, his eyes gleaming with malice.

Amid the heated debate, Cú Chulainn, though younger than the others, stood up and boldly declared that he would accept the challenge. His words silenced the room. Many of the older warriors doubted that Cú Chulainn, despite his reputation, could withstand the horrors that the Spancel Hoop would bring. But Cú Chulainn's resolve was unshakable. He was determined to prove himself once again, not just to his peers, but to himself and his king.

That night, Cú Chulainn took the Spancel Hoop and stood guard alone in the darkened hall. As the hours passed, the atmosphere grew tense, and the air seemed to thicken with an otherworldly presence. Then, as midnight approached, the hall was suddenly filled with terrifying apparitions—ghastly specters, hideous monsters, and fearsome beasts, all conjured by the power of the Spancel Hoop.

But Cú Chulainn did not flinch. His training, his innate courage, and the divine strength inherited from his father, Lugh, surged within him. He faced each apparition head-on, with his sword and spear flashing in the dim light. His movements were swift and precise, and his resolve was unwavering. As he battled the nightmarish foes, the other warriors, watching from a distance, could hardly believe what they saw.

The apparitions, though terrifying, were no match for Cú Chulainn's indomitable spirit. One by one, they were vanquished, until the hall was once again silent and still. The Spancel Hoop, its power spent, lay at Cú Chulainn's feet, and the young warrior stood victorious.

When dawn broke, the warriors of Ulster returned to the hall, expecting to find the place in ruins or worse, to discover that Cú Chulainn had fallen to the horrors of the night. Instead, they found him standing calmly, the Spancel Hoop in hand, and not a trace of fear or fatigue on his face. The warriors were awestruck, and even the most skeptical among them could not deny that Cú Chulainn had proven himself beyond doubt.

King Conchobar, deeply impressed by his nephew's bravery and skill, declared that Cú Chulainn was indeed the greatest hero of Ulster. The warriors, though some still harbored jealousy, could not dispute the king's judgment. Cú Chulainn had faced a test that none other could, and he had emerged triumphant.

The tale of the Spancel Hoop became another legend in the growing saga of Cú Chulainn's life. It was a story that would be told and retold around the fires of Emain Macha and throughout the lands of Ulster. It was a testament to his bravery, his unyielding spirit, and his destiny to become the greatest warrior of his time.

But this was only the beginning of Cú Chulainn's journey. The trials and battles that lay ahead would challenge him in ways he could not yet imagine. Each victory brought new challenges, and each challenge brought him closer to his fate as the Hound of Ulster. The gods themselves watched with interest, knowing that Cú Chulainn was not just a hero of men but a figure who would shape the very destiny of Ireland.

After his triumph with the Spancel Hoop, Cú Chulainn's fame as a warrior grew, spreading beyond the borders of Ulster. Yet, even with his growing renown, there was still one area of life in which he had yet to prove himself: love. The stories of Cú Chulainn often describe him as not just a fierce warrior but also a man of great beauty and charisma, traits that drew the attention of many women. However, Cú Chulainn's heart was set on one woman above all others—Emer, the daughter of Forgall Monach.

Emer was renowned throughout Ireland for her beauty, intelligence, and virtue. She was not easily won, and many suitors had already tried and failed to gain her favor. However, Cú Chulainn, ever determined, was not deterred by these challenges. He had heard of Emer's beauty and wisdom and felt that only she was worthy to be his wife. But Forgall, her father, was a cunning and ambitious man who sought to test Cú Chulainn's worth before allowing him to marry his daughter.

When Cú Chulainn first met Emer, he was immediately struck by her grace and intellect. Emer, too, was intrigued by Cú Chulainn, recognizing in him a warrior of unmatched skill and a man of strong character. However, she did not make her affections easy to obtain. Emer posed a series of riddles and challenges to Cú Chulainn, testing his wit and his understanding of the virtues that she held dear—courage, honor, and loyalty.

Cú Chulainn met each of these challenges with the same determination and brilliance he had shown in battle. His answers revealed not only his intelligence but also the depth of his character. Emer was impressed, but their union was far from secure. Forgall, determined to prevent the marriage, devised a plan to send Cú Chulainn on an almost impossible quest, hoping that he would be either killed or distracted long enough for Emer to marry another.

Forgall suggested that Cú Chulainn should travel to the land of Alba (Scotland) to train under the legendary warrior woman Scáthach, who was known for her mastery of martial arts and her ability to bestow incredible strength and skill upon those she trained. Scáthach's training was infamous for its rigor and danger, and many who sought her out never returned. Forgall believed that even if Cú Chulainn survived the training, it would take years, during which time Emer would surely marry someone else.

Undeterred by Forgall's scheme, Cú Chulainn embraced the challenge, seeing it as an opportunity to further prove his worthiness. He set out for Alba, journeying across the sea to the island fortress of Scáthach. The path to her fortress was treacherous, filled with physical obstacles and magical challenges designed to test the resolve of any who sought her teachings. But Cú Chulainn, with his divine strength and indomitable will, overcame every obstacle in his path.

When Cú Chulainn finally arrived at Scáthach's fortress, he was welcomed as a promising student. Scáthach recognized in him a kindred spirit, someone with the potential to surpass even her greatest students. Under her guidance, Cú Chulainn underwent rigorous training that pushed him to the limits of his abilities. He learned the use of the Gáe Bulg, a deadly spear that could only be mastered by the most skilled of warriors. He also learned techniques of combat that were beyond anything he had ever encountered, refining his already formidable skills to perfection.

During his time with Scáthach, Cú Chulainn also encountered another warrior woman named Aífe, who was Scáthach's rival. Aífe was as skilled and fierce as Scáthach, and the two had long been enemies. Cú Chulainn, always eager to test his strength, engaged Aífe in combat and defeated her, though he spared her life out of respect for her courage and skill. In return, Aífe bore him a son, Connla, whom Cú Chulainn would meet many years later under tragic circumstances.

After completing his training, Cú Chulainn returned to Ireland, his skills now honed to a level unmatched by any warrior in the land. He confronted Forgall Monach, who, despite his initial opposition, could no longer deny Cú Chulainn's worth. Cú Chulainn's victory over Forgall was not one of force but of undeniable prowess and honor, qualities that Emer herself valued above all else.

With Forgall's reluctant blessing, Cú Chulainn and Emer were finally wed. Their union was celebrated throughout Ulster, not just for the love they shared, but for the honor and courage that Cú Chulainn had displayed in winning her hand. Emer became Cú Chulainn's greatest support, and their marriage symbolized the unity of strength and wisdom, a partnership that would see Cú Chulainn through many of his future trials.

Yet, the life of a hero is never peaceful for long. Cú Chulainn's return to Ulster marked the beginning of a new chapter in his life, filled with battles, challenges, and the fulfillment of his destiny as the greatest warrior of Ireland. The lessons he had learned from Scáthach, and the love and wisdom he had found in Emer, would guide him as he faced the coming storms of war and conflict that would define his legendary career.

Cultural Significance and Context of "The Birth and Early Life of Cú Chulainn"

The tale of Cú Chulainn, particularly his birth and early life, is one of the most iconic and culturally significant stories in Irish mythology. As a central figure in the Ulster Cycle, Cú Chulainn embodies the archetype of the hero warrior, a symbol of strength, bravery, and tragic fate that resonates deeply with the Irish cultural identity. His story is rich in symbolic meaning, historical context, and has left a lasting impact on Irish literature, art, and national consciousness.

Cultural Significance

The Heroic Ideal

Cú Chulainn is often viewed as the quintessential hero in Irish mythology. His story parallels the hero's journey archetype found in many world mythologies—a young, seemingly ordinary boy who is revealed to have extraordinary abilities and a destiny that sets him apart. Cú Chulainn's feats of strength and courage from an early age align him with the heroic figures of other mythologies, such as Hercules in Greek mythology or Achilles in Homer's "Iliad."

However, Cú Chulainn's heroism is distinctively Irish in character. Unlike the often solitary heroes of other traditions, Cú Chulainn is deeply embedded within the social and cultural fabric of his community. His actions are motivated by loyalty to his kin, his king, and his homeland. This loyalty, combined with his superhuman abilities and tragic flaws, makes him a complex and relatable figure who embodies the values of courage, honor, and sacrifice.

The Divine and the Mortal

Cú Chulainn's birth is a fusion of the divine and the mortal, reflecting the deep interconnection between the human world and the otherworld in Irish mythology. His father, Lugh, is one of the most revered gods of the Tuatha Dé Danann, a race of divine beings who represent the pre-Christian gods of Ireland. By having a divine parent, Cú Chulainn's story bridges the gap between the mortal and the divine, allowing for the exploration of themes like fate, destiny, and the burden of greatness.

The dual nature of Cú Chulainn's heritage also reflects the broader cultural belief in the existence of otherworldly realms that influence the human world. The Tuatha Dé Danann, despite being displaced by the Milesians (the ancestors of the Irish people), continue to exert influence through their descendants, like Cú Chulainn. This connection emphasizes the belief in a world where the boundaries between the human and the supernatural are fluid and permeable.

The Importance of Names and Identity

Names hold great significance in Irish mythology, and the story of Cú Chulainn is no exception. His original name, Setanta, is associated with his childhood and ordinary beginnings, while the name Cú Chulainn, meaning "Hound of Culann," signifies his transformation into a hero. The act of naming in this context is both a rite of passage and a form of empowerment, marking the transition from youth to adulthood, from ordinary to extraordinary.

The name Cú Chulainn itself is rich in symbolism. In ancient Ireland, hounds were revered animals, representing loyalty, protection, and martial prowess. By taking on the name of the hound he killed, Cú Chulainn symbolically takes on the qualities of the hound—fearless, protective, and bound by a code of honor. This transformation is a key moment in his life, setting the stage for his future exploits and solidifying his identity as a hero.

The Role of Women and Gender Dynamics

The women in Cú Chulainn's life play pivotal roles in shaping his destiny. His mother, Dechtire, is central to the story of his conception and birth, embodying the archetypal role of the mother as both a nurturer and a conduit for divine intervention. Emer, his wife, represents wisdom and the ideal of feminine virtue in Irish mythology. Their relationship is one of mutual respect and partnership, reflecting the importance of wisdom and loyalty in a warrior's life.

Scáthach, the warrior woman who trains Cú Chulainn, is another significant female figure. She represents a different aspect of the feminine, one that is strong, skilled, and independent. In training Cú Chulainn, Scáthach bestows upon him not only martial skills but also a deeper understanding of what it means to be a warrior. Her role underscores the idea that true heroism involves not just physical strength but also mental and spiritual fortitude.

Historical and Mythological Context

The Ulster Cycle

Cú Chulainn's story is part of the Ulster Cycle, one of the four major cycles of Irish mythology. The Ulster Cycle is set during the heroic age of Ulster and tells the stories of the Red Branch Knights, the warriors who served under King Conchobar mac Nessa. These tales are rooted in a pre-Christian, Iron Age Ireland, reflecting the values, social structures, and conflicts of that time.

The Ulster Cycle is characterized by its focus on the themes of honor, loyalty, and the warrior ethos. It portrays a society where kinship and loyalty to one's lord and people are paramount, and where personal honor must be upheld at all costs. Cú Chulainn, as the central hero of the Ulster Cycle, embodies these values to an extreme degree, often at great personal cost.

The Influence of Celtic and Indo-European Mythology

The story of Cú Chulainn is deeply influenced by Celtic mythology and shares common elements with other Indo-European heroic traditions. The figure of the hero who undergoes a rite of passage, gains supernatural abilities, and faces numerous challenges is a recurring motif in many cultures. However, Cú Chulainn's story is uniquely Irish in its integration of the land, the otherworld, and the deep connection to the warrior ethos of the Celtic people.

Cú Chulainn's ríastrad, or warp-spasm, where he undergoes a terrifying transformation in battle, has parallels with the berserkers of Norse mythology and the idea of divine frenzy in other Indo-European traditions. This transformation symbolizes the unleashing of the hero's full potential, often with destructive consequences, reflecting the ambivalence of heroism—its capacity for both creation and destruction.

Literary and Artistic Impact

Irish Literature and Oral Tradition

Cú Chulainn's story has been passed down through generations, originally through the oral tradition of the filid (poets) and later through written manuscripts like the "Táin Bó Cúailnge" (The Cattle Raid of Cooley). This epic, in which Cú Chulainn plays a central role, is often compared to other great epics like the "Iliad" and the "Aeneid" in its scope and significance.

The tales of Cú Chulainn have inspired countless poets, writers, and storytellers over the centuries. During the Irish Literary Revival of the late 19th and early 20th centuries, figures like W.B. Yeats and Lady Gregory drew heavily on the Ulster Cycle in their efforts to revive and celebrate Ireland's literary heritage. Cú Chulainn became a symbol of the Irish nationalist movement, representing the spirit of resistance and the struggle for independence.

Visual Arts and Popular Culture

Cú Chulainn's story has also been a rich source of inspiration for visual artists. The image of the young hero, often depicted in the midst of his warp-spasm or engaged in battle, has appeared in paintings, sculptures, and stained glass windows throughout Ireland. His iconic status as a symbol of Irish heroism is reflected in public monuments, such as the statue of Cú Chulainn at the General Post Office in Dublin, which commemorates the 1916 Easter Rising.

In modern times, Cú Chulainn has continued to inspire works of fiction, film, and even video games, where his story is reimagined and adapted for contemporary audiences. These adaptations often explore the timeless themes of his myth, such as the tension between duty and personal desire, the costs of heroism, and the nature of fate.

Symbolism and Themes

The Heroic Tragedy

One of the most enduring aspects of Cú Chulainn's story is its tragic dimension. Despite his extraordinary abilities and his status as a hero, Cú Chulainn is often portrayed as a figure doomed by his own greatness. His heroism isolates him, setting him apart from his peers and making him a target for the machinations of both gods and men. This tragic element adds depth to his character, making him a hero not just of physical might but of moral and existential struggle.

The prophecy that surrounds Cú Chulainn's life—that he would be the greatest hero of his time, but that his life would be short—casts a shadow over his story from the beginning. This tension between glory and doom is a central theme in his narrative, reflecting the broader human experience of striving for greatness while being bound by the limitations of mortality.

The Warrior's Code and Sacrifice

Cú Chulainn's story is also a reflection on the warrior's code—a set of values that prioritize honor, loyalty, and courage above all else. In Cú Chulainn's world, these values are non-negotiable, and the consequences of violating them are severe. His adherence to this code, even when it leads to personal loss and tragedy, underscores the importance of integrity and duty in the warrior ethos.

The theme of sacrifice is woven throughout Cú Chulainn's life.

He sacrifices his childhood, his personal happiness, and ultimately his life for the sake of his people and his honor. This idea of sacrifice is deeply embedded in Irish culture, reflecting a long history of struggle and resilience in the face of adversity.

Conclusion

The birth and early life of Cú Chulainn is more than just a story of a boy who becomes a warrior; it is a narrative that encapsulates the core values and beliefs of ancient Irish society. It speaks to the universal themes of heroism, sacrifice, and the interplay between fate and free will, while also reflecting the unique cultural and mythological context of Ireland. Cú Chulainn's story has endured for centuries, continuing to inspire and resonate with audiences as a powerful symbol of the Irish spirit, both in its strength and its capacity for profound, tragic beauty. Through the lens of his life, we gain insight into the cultural psyche of Ireland, where the past and the mythic still hold a profound influence on the present.

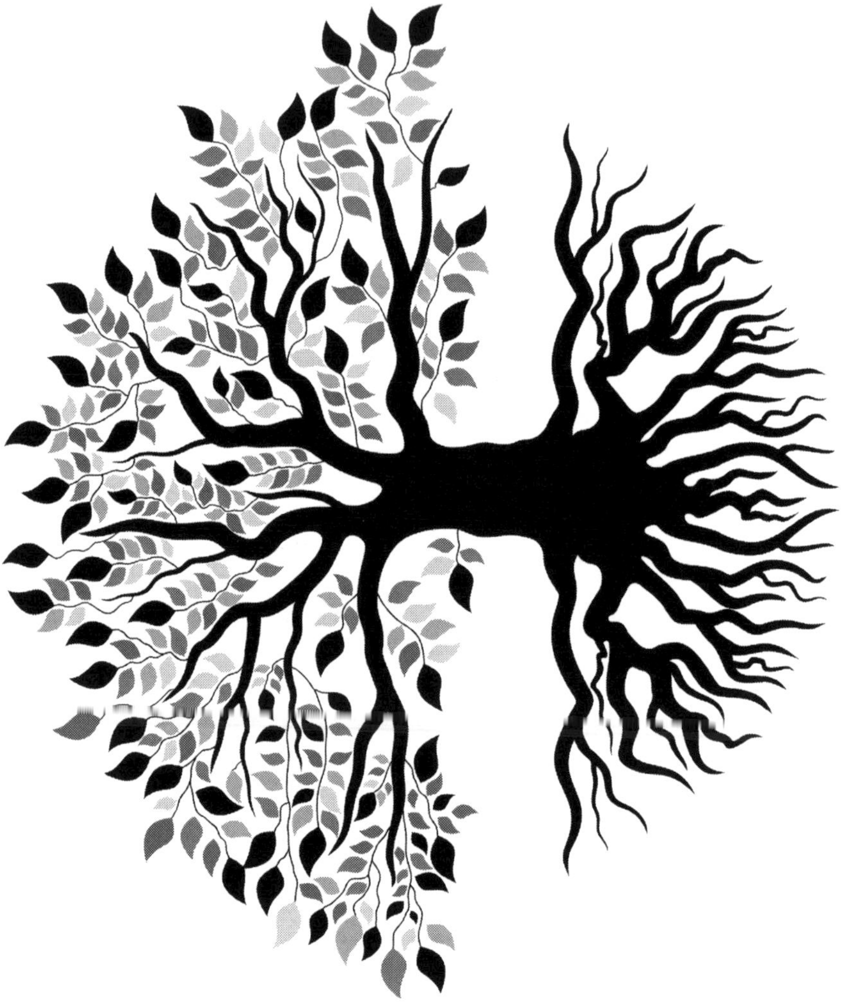

The Tale of The Salmon of Knowledge

Long ago, in the mystical land of ancient Ireland, a land where the boundary between the human and the divine was thin, and where the rivers, forests, and hills were filled with magic, there was a prophecy that spoke of a fish—no ordinary fish, but a Salmon of Knowledge. This salmon, it was said, would one day be caught, and whoever first tasted its flesh would gain all the wisdom of the world.

The Salmon of Knowledge lived in the sacred waters of the River Boyne, a river that was itself steeped in legend and revered by the people. The salmon was said to have eaten the nine hazelnuts that had fallen into the river from nine ancient hazel trees surrounding a sacred well, the Well of Wisdom. These hazelnuts contained all the knowledge of the world, and by consuming them, the salmon had become imbued with immeasurable wisdom.

The story of the Salmon of Knowledge was well-known among the people of Ireland, particularly among the druids, the wise men and keepers of ancient lore. It was believed that whoever consumed the flesh of this salmon would gain insight into all things—past, present, and future—and would possess

F.T. Weaver

the wisdom to lead, to heal, and to understand the mysteries of the universe.

In a time when kings and warriors often sought the counsel of druids, the pursuit of wisdom was as important as the pursuit of power. The tales of great heroes and leaders often began with a quest for knowledge, for it was understood that true leadership required not only strength and courage but also the wisdom to guide others.

Among those who sought the Salmon of Knowledge was a druid named Finegas. Finegas was a man of great learning and deep meditation, who had spent many years living by the banks of the River Boyne, studying its waters and seeking the elusive salmon. He knew the old prophecies and believed with all his heart that his destiny was to catch the Salmon of Knowledge and gain the wisdom that it possessed.

Finegas was not a man of haste; he understood that the pursuit of knowledge was a slow and patient endeavor. Day after day, he fished in the Boyne, using all the skills he had learned over a lifetime dedicated to the study of the natural world. Though many years passed, and though he grew older and more weathered with each passing season, he did not abandon his quest. He continued to fish, to observe, and to wait for the day when the Salmon of Knowledge would reveal itself to him.

Meanwhile, across the land of Ireland, a young boy named Fionn mac Cumhaill was growing up, unaware of the destiny that awaited him. Fionn was the son of Cumhall, a great warrior who had died in battle before Fionn was born, and Muirne, his mother. After his father's death, Fionn was raised in secret by two wise women, Bodhmall and Liath Luachra, who taught him the skills of a warrior and the ways of the wild. Fionn grew up strong and agile, with a keen mind and a brave heart, but he was also curious and eager to learn more about the world.

As Fionn reached his teenage years, he set out on his own, traveling across Ireland, seeking knowledge and adventure. He had heard tales of the great warriors and leaders of old, and he knew that if he was to follow in their footsteps, he needed to acquire not just strength, but wisdom. His journey eventually led him to the banks of the River Boyne, where he met the old druid Finegas.

Finegas, though he had lived alone for many years, recognized something special in the young Fionn. There was a spark in his eyes, a hunger for knowledge that resonated with Finegas's own lifelong quest. Fionn, in turn, was drawn to the old druid, sensing that this was a man who could teach him much about the world.

Fionn offered to serve Finegas, to help him with his daily tasks and to learn from him in return. Finegas accepted, seeing in Fionn not just a willing student, but perhaps the fulfillment of the prophecy that had guided his life for so long. Together, they fished, they talked, and Finegas shared with Fionn the stories and secrets of the land, the stars, and the ancient traditions of the druids.

Though Finegas had spent many years in solitude, his time with Fionn brought him a renewed sense of purpose. He could see that Fionn was destined for greatness, and he was eager to impart as much knowledge as he could to the young man. Yet, Finegas also knew that his own quest was not yet complete. He still awaited the day when the Salmon of Knowledge would reveal itself, and he would finally gain the wisdom he had sought for so long.

Fionn, meanwhile, continued to learn and grow under Finegas's guidance. He absorbed the old druid's teachings with enthusiasm, and his understanding of the world deepened with each passing day. Yet, despite all he learned, Fionn was unaware of the role that destiny had chosen for him in the story of the Salmon of Knowledge.

Finegas had lived by the River Boyne for many years, his days marked by a patient, unwavering commitment to his quest for the Salmon of Knowledge. Despite the passage of time and the wear of age, his spirit remained as resolute as ever. He was a man of quiet wisdom, his life a testament to the idea that true knowledge comes not just from books or teachings, but from a deep connection with the world and its mysteries.

Each day, Finegas would rise before dawn, his old bones creaking as he prepared his fishing gear. He would walk to the riverbank, where the mist hung low over the water like a shroud, and cast his line into the flowing current. The river was his companion, its waters whispering ancient secrets that only a druid like Finegas could hear. He had come to know every bend and eddy, every rock and pool, and he was certain that the Salmon of Knowledge still swam within its depths.

Though he had never seen the salmon, Finegas had heard tales of its shimmering scales and the light that seemed to emanate from within it. He knew that the salmon was no ordinary fish; it was a creature of magic and wisdom, blessed by the gods themselves. The hazelnuts it had consumed were said to hold the essence of all knowledge, the very thoughts of the universe condensed into a single, perfect form.

Over the years, many had sought the Salmon of Knowledge, but none had succeeded. Some had given up, deeming the task impossible, while others had dismissed the tale as mere legend. But Finegas, with his druidic insight, knew better. He could feel the presence of the salmon in the river, a subtle energy that had kept him anchored to this place for so long.

One crisp autumn morning, as the leaves began to turn

golden and the air held a slight chill, Finegas set out for the river as he had done countless times before. But this morning felt different. There was a stillness in the air, a sense of anticipation that set his heart racing with a hope he had not felt in years.

As Finegas reached the river, he noticed a faint glimmer beneath the surface of the water. He squinted, trying to see through the shifting reflections of the morning sun, and then he saw it—the Salmon of Knowledge. It was as magnificent as the legends had described, its scales glistening with a silvery sheen, its movements graceful and deliberate as it swam against the current.

Finegas's hands trembled as he cast his line into the water, careful to keep his movements slow and steady. The salmon, seemingly aware of his presence, approached the bait with a calm deliberation. Time seemed to slow as Finegas watched the fish, his breath held in his chest. Then, with a swift motion, the salmon took the bait, and Finegas felt a sharp tug on his line.

Years of experience guided Finegas as he worked to reel in the fish, his focus unwavering despite the adrenaline that surged through him. The salmon fought with a strength that belied its size, but Finegas was determined. He had waited a lifetime for this moment, and he would not let it slip away.

Finally, after what felt like an eternity, Finegas pulled the salmon from the water. It lay before him, its scales shimmering like a pool of liquid silver, its eyes reflecting the light of the rising sun. Finegas stared at the fish, his heart pounding with a mixture of triumph and awe. He had done it—he had caught the Salmon of Knowledge.

With the salmon secured, Finegas carefully wrapped it in a cloth and began the journey back to his small hut by the river. His mind was a whirl of thoughts and emotions, the weight of what he had accomplished pressing down on him like a physical force. He knew that this fish held the wisdom he had sought for so long, but he also knew that the prophecy was clear—the first to taste its flesh would gain that wisdom.

As he reached his hut, Finegas paused, looking down at the salmon in his hands. He had spent his life in pursuit of this moment, and now that it was here, he felt a strange sense of uncertainty. The wisdom he sought was within his grasp, yet something held him back.

It was at that moment that Fionn, the young warrior who had come to study under Finegas, returned from his own morning tasks. Fionn, who had been gathering firewood, saw the expression on Finegas's face and knew that something extraordinary had happened.

"What is it, Master?" Fionn asked, his eyes filled with curiosity.

Finegas looked at Fionn, the boy who had become like a son to him, and felt a pang of something he could not quite name. He knew the prophecy, knew that Fionn's arrival at this precise moment was no coincidence. The gods, it seemed, had woven their own design into the fabric of this story, and Finegas was but a part of it.

"I have caught the Salmon of Knowledge," Finegas said, his voice a mixture of pride and resignation. "But I need you to cook it for me. Be careful, though—make sure you do not eat any of it. The wisdom it holds is meant for me."

Fionn nodded, understanding the importance of the task. He respected Finegas and had no intention of disobeying him. He took the salmon and prepared it for cooking, building a fire outside the hut and setting the fish on a spit over the flames.

As the salmon cooked, Fionn tended to it carefully, turning the spit to ensure it was evenly roasted. The smell of the fish filled the air, rich and enticing, and Fionn found himself drawn to it, though he kept Finegas's warning in mind.

However, as Fionn worked, a small blister formed on the skin of the salmon, popping and releasing a drop of hot oil onto his thumb. Instinctively, Fionn raised his thumb to his mouth to soothe the burn, tasting the fish for the briefest of moments.

In that instant, everything changed. Fionn felt a rush of clarity, a sudden expansion of his mind as if a veil had been lifted from his understanding. The world around him seemed to sharpen, the colors brighter, the sounds clearer. He looked at the salmon, realizing what had happened, and a sense of both awe and fear filled him.

When the salmon was fully cooked, Fionn brought it to Finegas, who had been waiting patiently inside the hut. Finegas took one look at Fionn and knew, without a word being spoken, what had occurred. The light in Fionn's eyes, the calm composure he now carried—it was clear that the boy had tasted the salmon and gained its wisdom.

Finegas was silent for a long moment, his heart heavy with the realization that the prophecy had been fulfilled, but not in the way he had expected. The wisdom he had sought for so long was not meant for him, but for Fionn, the young warrior who would one day lead Ireland's greatest warriors.

Finally, Finegas smiled, a small, bittersweet smile. "Tell me, Fionn," he said, "did you eat of the salmon?"

Fionn, understanding the gravity of the moment, nodded. "I did not mean to, Master. A drop of oil burned my thumb, and I tasted it without thinking."

Finegas nodded, accepting the truth with the wisdom he had cultivated over a lifetime. "It is as it was meant to be," he said gently. "The knowledge was not mine to take. You are destined for greatness, Fionn mac Cumhaill. The wisdom of the salmon was meant for you."

With those words, the relationship between Finegas and Fionn shifted. Finegas knew that his role as a teacher had come to an end, and that Fionn was now equipped with the wisdom to fulfill his destiny. There was no bitterness in Finegas's heart, only a deep sense of peace, knowing that he had played his part in the unfolding of a story much larger than himself.

As Finegas gazed at Fionn, he could see the subtle but profound transformation that had taken place in the young man. There was a new depth in Fionn's eyes, a quiet understanding that spoke of knowledge far beyond his years. Finegas had devoted his life to the pursuit of wisdom, and now, before him, stood the embodiment of that quest, fulfilled in the most unexpected way.

Fionn, though aware of the change within himself, remained humble in the face of this newfound wisdom. He respected Finegas deeply and was concerned about how the druid would react to the accident that had led to Fionn's tasting of the salmon. But Finegas, with the clarity that comes from a life of contemplation, was not angry. Instead, he was accepting, for he understood that fate often works in ways that are beyond human comprehension.

"Young Fionn," Finegas said with a gentle tone, "there is no need for guilt or regret. The Salmon of Knowledge is a creature of prophecy, and its destiny, like yours, was written long ago. The gods have chosen you, and I see now that my role was to prepare you for this moment."

Fionn felt a deep sense of gratitude toward Finegas. He knew that without the druid's guidance, he would not have been ready to receive the wisdom that had come to him. He also recognized that this moment was a turning point in his life—a moment that would shape his future and the future of Ireland.

Folk Tales from Ireland

"Thank you, Master Finegas," Fionn said, his voice steady but filled with emotion. "You have given me more than I could have ever asked for. I will carry your teachings with me always."

Finegas nodded, acknowledging the bond that had formed between them. He knew that Fionn's journey was just beginning, and that the young warrior would need all the wisdom he had gained to navigate the challenges that lay ahead.

With the meal of the salmon now before them, Finegas invited Fionn to share in the food. Though Finegas knew that the wisdom was already imparted to Fionn, he still partook in the meal as a symbolic act, acknowledging the completion of his own quest. Together, they ate in silence, each man lost in his thoughts.

After the meal, Finegas sat back, his old eyes twinkling with a mixture of pride and nostalgia. He had devoted his life to a single goal, and though he had not achieved it in the way he had imagined, he felt a deep satisfaction in knowing that his efforts had not been in vain.

"Fionn," Finegas began after a long pause, "you are now equipped with the knowledge of the world. But remember, wisdom is not just about knowing—it is about understanding how to use that knowledge. The decisions you make, the paths you choose, will define the kind of leader you will become."

Fionn listened intently, absorbing Finegas's words with the same reverence he had always shown. The wisdom he had gained from the salmon was vast, but he knew that Finegas's counsel was invaluable, providing him with the perspective he needed to harness his newfound insight.

"You will face many challenges, Fionn," Finegas continued. "There will be times when your strength and courage are tested, and there will be moments when the wisdom you now possess will be the only thing that guides you. Trust in yourself, but also trust in the lessons you have learned from those who have come before you."

Fionn nodded, understanding the weight of the responsibility that now rested on his shoulders. He was no longer just a warrior seeking knowledge—he was now a custodian of wisdom, tasked with using it to protect and lead his people.

As the evening drew on, Fionn and Finegas shared stories and memories, their bond deepened by the knowledge that their paths would soon diverge. Finegas, content with the role he had played in shaping Fionn's destiny, felt a sense of peace that he had not known before. He had spent so many years in pursuit of the salmon, and now that the quest was complete, he could rest, knowing that his life's work had borne fruit.

The following morning, Fionn prepared to leave Finegas's hut, ready to embark on the next stage of his journey. Finegas, though saddened to see him go, knew that this was the natural course of things. The old druid gave Fionn a final blessing, wishing him strength, courage, and the clarity to use his wisdom wisely.

"Go forth, Fionn mac Cumhaill," Finegas said, placing a hand on Fionn's shoulder. "You are destined for greatness, but greatness carries with it a heavy burden. May the knowledge you have gained guide you well, and may you always remember the lessons of humility and honor."

Fionn, deeply moved by Finegas's words, embraced the old druid. "I will not forget," he promised. "I will carry your teachings with me, wherever I go."

With that, Fionn departed, leaving the tranquil banks of the River Boyne and setting out into the wider world. The wisdom he had gained from the Salmon of Knowledge was like a beacon, illuminating the path before him. He knew that he would face many trials, but he also knew that he was ready to meet them, armed with the knowledge that few others possessed.

As he traveled, Fionn's reputation as a warrior and leader began to grow. He joined the ranks of the Fianna, the legendary band of warriors who served the High King of Ireland, and quickly rose to prominence. His wisdom, combined with his physical prowess and tactical brilliance, set him apart from his peers.

In time, Fionn became the leader of the Fianna, guiding them through countless battles and adventures. His decisions were always tempered by the wisdom he had gained from the Salmon of Knowledge, allowing him to navigate complex situations with insight and clarity. Under his leadership, the Fianna became a force to be reckoned with, feared by their enemies and revered by their allies.

But Fionn never forgot the lessons of humility and honor that Finegas had imparted to him. He led with compassion as well as strength, always seeking to protect the innocent and uphold justice. His wisdom allowed him to see beyond the immediate challenges, to understand the long-term consequences of his actions, and to make decisions that would benefit not just himself, but all of Ireland.

Cultural Significance and Other Cultural Facts About "The Salmon of Knowledge"

"The Salmon of Knowledge" is a tale deeply embedded in Irish mythology, a story that not only reflects the rich cultural heritage of Ireland but also encapsulates themes of wisdom, destiny, and the transmission of knowledge across generations. The tale is part of the larger mythological framework surrounding Fionn mac Cumhaill, a legendary figure who plays a central role in many Irish myths and whose story has been passed down

through oral tradition for centuries. Understanding the cultural significance of this tale requires exploring its symbolic meanings, its place within Irish mythology, and its influence on Irish literature and culture.

Cultural Significance

The Quest for Knowledge

At the heart of the story is the theme of the quest for knowledge—a concept that holds immense cultural value in Irish mythology and, more broadly, in Celtic traditions. The Salmon of Knowledge, having gained its wisdom by consuming the hazelnuts from the Well of Wisdom, symbolizes the ultimate attainment of understanding, insight, and enlightenment. This well, also known as Connla's Well, is one of the many sacred wells in Irish mythology, representing a source of divine knowledge and inspiration.

The pursuit of this knowledge is not a simple or straightforward journey. It requires patience, dedication, and often, a deep connection with nature and the spiritual world. Finegas, the druid who devotes his life to catching the Salmon of Knowledge, embodies this pursuit. His quest reflects the broader druidic tradition in ancient Ireland, where knowledge was revered, and the acquisition of wisdom was seen as a lifelong endeavor.

The idea that wisdom is a treasure to be sought after is a recurring motif in many cultures, but in Irish mythology, it is particularly associated with the natural world and the idea that true knowledge comes from understanding the deeper truths of life and the universe. The salmon, a creature of the river, represents a bridge between the physical and the metaphysical, between the world of men and the realm of the gods.

Symbolism of the Salmon

The salmon itself is a potent symbol in Celtic mythology. Fish, particularly salmon, are often associated with knowledge and prophecy in various mythological traditions. In the Irish context, the salmon is closely tied to the concept of transformation and enlightenment. By consuming the hazelnuts that fall into the Well of Wisdom, the salmon becomes a vessel of divine knowledge, embodying the idea that true wisdom comes from the natural world, which is imbued with the sacred.

The salmon's journey from the well to the river can also be seen as a metaphor for the dissemination of knowledge from the divine or mystical realms to the mortal world. This journey echoes the broader theme of the passage of knowledge through time and across generations, highlighting the importance of learning and wisdom in sustaining cultural continuity.

The act of catching the Salmon of Knowledge is not just a physical task but a spiritual quest. It requires more than just skill—it demands patience, reverence, and a deep understanding of the natural world. Finegas's life by the river, spent in meditation and quiet observation, reflects the druidic belief in the importance of living in harmony with nature and being attuned to its rhythms and secrets.

The Role of Fate and Destiny

The story of Fionn mac Cumhaill and the Salmon of Knowledge is also a tale about fate and destiny. From the moment Finegas catches the salmon, it is clear that a greater force is at work. The prophecy that whoever eats the salmon will gain all the knowledge of the world suggests that certain events are predestined, beyond the control of the individuals involved.

Fionn's accidental consumption of the salmon's oil, which grants him the knowledge, can be seen as a moment of destiny. Despite Finegas's efforts to attain the wisdom for himself, the universe has other plans, and it is Fionn who is meant to inherit the knowledge. This aspect of the story reflects a broader theme in Irish mythology, where fate is often seen as an inevitable force that guides the lives of heroes and mortals alike.

The story also touches on the idea that wisdom and leadership are divinely ordained. Fionn's rise to prominence as a leader of the Fianna, following his acquisition of the salmon's wisdom, suggests that his destiny was to lead and protect Ireland, and that the knowledge he gains is what equips him to fulfill this role. In this way, the tale reinforces the idea that true leaders are chosen by fate and endowed with the qualities needed to guide their people.

Place in Irish Mythology

The Fenian Cycle

The story of the Salmon of Knowledge is part of the Fenian Cycle (also known as the Fiannaíocht), one of the four major cycles of Irish mythology. This cycle is centered around the hero Fionn mac Cumhaill and the Fianna, a band of warriors who served as protectors of the High King of Ireland. The Fenian Cycle is filled with tales of heroism, adventure, and romance, and it holds a special place in Irish folklore for its emphasis on the values of loyalty, bravery, and wisdom.

Fionn mac Cumhaill is one of the most celebrated figures in Irish mythology, and his stories have been passed down through generations, both in oral tradition and in written form. The Salmon of Knowledge tale serves as an origin story for Fionn, explaining how he came to possess the extraordinary wisdom that would define his leadership and his place in Irish legend.

In the broader context of the Fenian Cycle, the story highlights the importance of mentorship and the transmission of knowledge. Finegas's role as a mentor to Fionn, even though it is Fionn who ultimately gains the knowledge, underscores the idea that wisdom is passed from one generation to the next, and that the younger generation often carries forward the legacy of their elders.

The Druidic Tradition

The character of Finegas is deeply connected to the druidic tradition in Ireland. Druids were the learned class of ancient Celtic society, responsible for religious rites, law, and the transmission of knowledge. They were considered intermediaries between the mortal world and the divine, possessing a deep understanding of nature, spirituality, and the mysteries of the universe.

Finegas's life by the River Boyne, his patient quest for the Salmon of Knowledge, and his acceptance of Fionn's destiny all reflect the druidic values of wisdom, humility, and reverence for the natural world. The druidic tradition emphasized that true knowledge could not be rushed or forced—it had to be earned through years of study, observation, and spiritual practice.

In this context, Finegas represents the ideal druid—wise, patient, and devoted to his quest for understanding. His willingness to accept Fionn's accidental attainment of the salmon's wisdom reflects the druidic belief in fate and the idea that the universe unfolds according to its own mysterious plan.

Influence on Irish Literature and Culture

Oral Tradition and Storytelling

The story of the Salmon of Knowledge has been preserved through Ireland's rich oral storytelling tradition. For centuries, it has been told by seanchaí (traditional storytellers) in homes, at gatherings, and in bardic schools, where it was passed down from generation to generation. This oral tradition has kept the story alive, allowing it to evolve and adapt while retaining its core themes and messages.

The tale's enduring popularity is a testament to its universal appeal and its ability to convey important cultural values in an engaging and memorable way. The story's emphasis on the pursuit of knowledge, the importance of mentorship, and the role of destiny resonates with audiences across time, making it a staple of Irish folklore.

Literary Revival and National Identity

During the Irish Literary Revival of the late 19th and early 20th centuries, the story of the Salmon of Knowledge, along with other tales from the Fenian Cycle, was rediscovered and celebrated by Irish writers and poets. Figures such as W.B. Yeats, Lady Gregory, and James Stephens drew on these ancient myths to create works that reflected Ireland's cultural heritage and national identity.

The story of Fionn and the Salmon of Knowledge was particularly appealing to these writers because of its themes of wisdom, leadership, and the connection between the past and the present. In a time when Ireland was seeking to assert its cultural independence and reclaim its heritage, the tale served as a powerful reminder of the country's ancient traditions and the enduring importance of knowledge and wisdom.

The mythological landscape of Ireland, with its sacred wells, enchanted rivers, and wise druids, became a source of inspiration for these writers, who saw in these stories a way to connect the Irish people with their roots and to create a sense of pride in their shared history and culture.

Symbolism and Themes

The Relationship Between Knowledge and Power

One of the central themes of the Salmon of Knowledge story is the relationship between knowledge and power. Fionn's acquisition of the salmon's wisdom is not just about gaining insight—it is about gaining the power to lead and protect his *people. In this way, the story suggests that true power comes from knowledge, and that those who possess wisdom are best equipped to wield authority.*

This theme is deeply embedded in Irish culture, where leaders were often expected to be not just warriors but also sages who could guide their people with wisdom and foresight. The tale reinforces the idea that leadership is not just about physical strength or martial prowess—it is about the ability to understand the world, to make informed decisions, and to act in the best interests of the community.

The Sacredness of Nature

The Salmon of Knowledge story is also a celebration of the sacredness of nature, a theme that is central to Celtic spirituality. The salmon, the River Boyne, and the Well of Wisdom are all depicted as sacred, imbued with divine energy and significance. This reflects the Celtic belief that the natural world is alive with spirit and that certain places and creatures hold special power.

The story encourages a deep reverence for nature, suggesting that wisdom and knowledge are not found in isolation from the world, but are intimately connected to the land, the water, and the living beings that inhabit them. This theme resonates with the modern environmental movement, which often looks to indigenous and ancient traditions for models of living in harmony with the earth.

The Mentor-Student Relationship

The relationship between Finegas and Fionn is another key theme of the story, highlighting the importance of mentorship and the transmission of knowledge. Finegas, as Fionn's mentor, represents the older generation of wisdom keepers who pass on their knowledge to the next generation. This relationship is depicted with great respect and reverence, emphasizing the idea that learning is a lifelong process and that true wisdom comes from both teaching and being taught.

The story also explores the idea that wisdom is not just something that can be imparted—it is something that must be experienced and internalized. Fionn's accidental taste of the salmon's oil represents the moment when he internalizes the knowledge that Finegas has been teaching him, making it his own.

Conclusion

The story of "The Salmon of Knowledge" is a rich and multifaceted tale that has deep roots in Irish mythology and culture. It speaks to universal themes of the quest for knowledge, the role of fate and destiny, and the importance of mentorship and the sacredness of nature. Its influence on Irish literature, oral tradition, and national identity is profound, making it one of the most enduring and celebrated stories in the Irish cultural canon.

Through the story of Fionn mac Cumhaill and the Salmon of Knowledge, we gain insight into the values and beliefs of ancient Ireland, where wisdom was revered, nature was sacred, and the journey to understanding was seen as one of life's greatest adventures. The tale continues to resonate with audiences today, offering timeless lessons about the pursuit of knowledge, the responsibilities of leadership, and the power of destiny in shaping our lives.

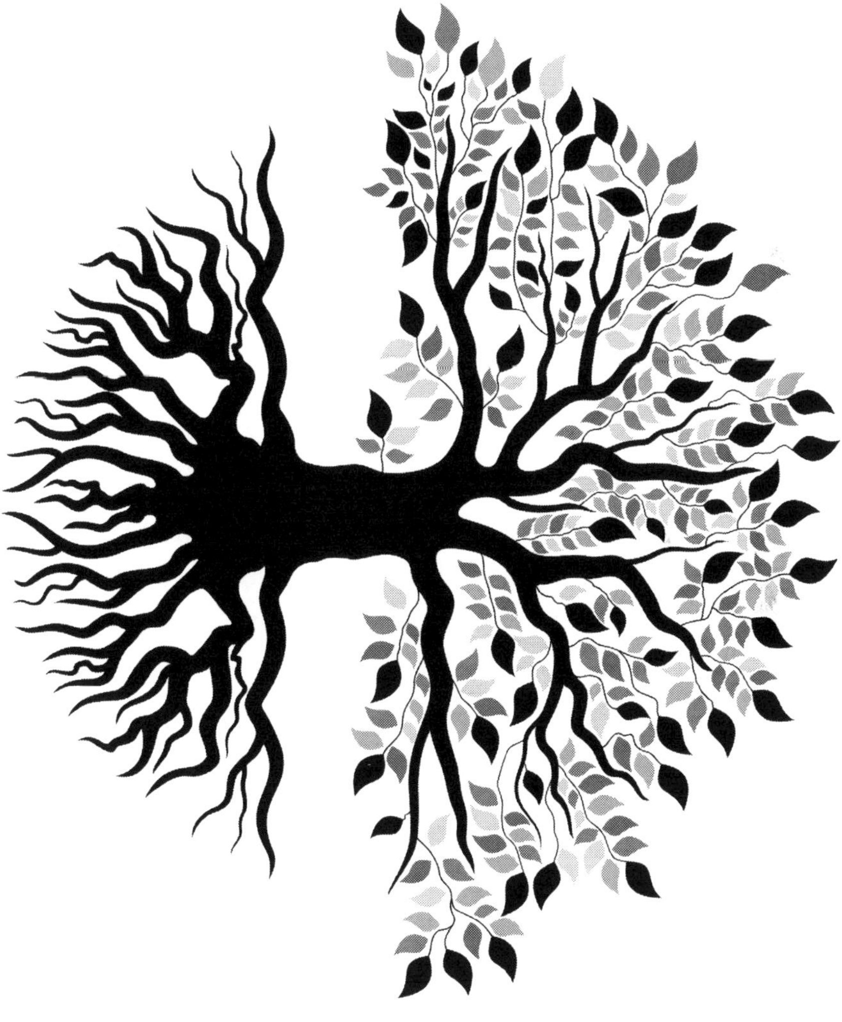

The Tale of The Tuatha Dé Danann

In the ancient mists of time, before the world as we know it took shape, Ireland was a land filled with magic and mystery, where the veil between the mortal world and the Otherworld was thin. It was during this primordial age that the Tuatha Dé Danann, a divine race of gods and magical beings, arrived on the shores of Ireland, forever altering the destiny of the land and its people.

The Tuatha Dé Danann were not of this world, but came from distant, mystical realms beyond the sea. They were a people of great beauty, wisdom, and power, often described as beings who shone with an inner light. Their name, which means "People of the Goddess Danu," reflects their connection to the goddess Danu, the mother figure of their race. Danu was the embodiment of the earth and the waters, the source of life and fertility, and it was from her that the Tuatha Dé Danann drew their strength and vitality.

Legends say that the Tuatha Dé Danann arrived in Ireland on a day shrouded in mist, descending from the skies in great, dark clouds. Some stories suggest they arrived in ships that they burned upon landing, so they could not be used again—indicating their intention to remain in Ireland as their new home. Their arrival was marked by a magical storm that obscured the sun for three days and three nights, heralding their entrance into the world.

The Tuatha Dé Danann were skilled in all forms of art and science. They were masters of magic, capable of altering the natural world with their spells and enchantments. They brought with them four great treasures, each one imbued with extraordinary powers. These treasures were:

The Stone of Fal (Lia Fáil): A sacred stone that would roar when touched by the rightful king of Ireland.

The Spear of Lugh: A weapon that was said to be unstoppable in battle, ensuring victory to its wielder.

The Sword of Nuada (Claíomh Solais): A sword that could cut through any enemy, said to be invincible.

The Cauldron of Dagda: A cauldron that could provide endless sustenance, never leaving anyone unsatisfied.

These treasures were not just symbols of their power, but also represented the divine right to rule, wisdom, and the sustenance of life—qualities that the Tuatha Dé Danann would embody during their time in Ireland.

Upon their arrival, the Tuatha Dé Danann found that Ireland was not an empty land, but was already inhabited by a race known as the Fir Bolg, a people who had settled the land before them. The Fir Bolg were hardy and strong, descendants of an earlier race of settlers, and they ruled over Ireland with a stern hand.

The arrival of the Tuatha Dé Danann was met with suspicion and hostility by the Fir Bolg, who saw them as invaders threatening their dominion over the land. However, the Tuatha Dé Danann, despite their superior knowledge and magic, did not immediately seek to conquer the Fir Bolg. They desired peace and wished to share the land rather than take it by force.

A meeting was arranged between the leaders of the two peoples to discuss terms of cohabitation. The Tuatha Dé Danann sent their king, Nuada, a wise and fair ruler, to negotiate with the Fir Bolg. Nuada proposed that the land be divided equally between the two races, allowing both to live and prosper in harmony. However, the Fir Bolg, proud and wary of losing their sovereignty, refused this offer.

Unable to reach an agreement, the only course left was war. The Fir Bolg, despite their fear of the Tuatha Dé Danann's magical abilities, prepared for battle, determined to defend their land. The Tuatha Dé Danann, though reluctant to shed blood, accepted the necessity of battle to secure their place in Ireland.

Thus began the first great battle of Ireland's mythological history, the Battle of Mag Tuired, where the Tuatha Dé Danann would face the Fir Bolg to determine the fate of the land. This battle would be the first test of the Tuatha Dé Danann's might, a clash that would set the stage for their reign and their interactions with the other ancient races of Ireland.

As the Tuatha Dé Danann prepared for battle, their warriors and sorcerers made ready their arms and spells, and their leaders invoked the blessings of the goddess Danu. The Fir Bolg, resolute and fierce, gathered their own warriors, prepared to defend their home against the divine newcomers.

The outcome of this battle would not only determine the fate of Ireland but would also shape the legends that would be told for generations to come, tales of gods and heroes, of magic and might, that would echo through the annals of Irish history.

The day of the battle dawned with a heavy sky, the air thick with anticipation. The Tuatha Dé Danann, with their ethereal beauty and unmatched skills in magic and warfare, stood ready to face the Fir Bolg on the plains of Mag Tuired. This battlefield, destined to become a place of legend, would be the site of a conflict that would echo through the ages.

The Fir Bolg were no strangers to war. They were a hardy people, descended from the earlier inhabitants of Ireland, and they had carved out a life in this rugged land through sheer determination and strength. Their warriors were fierce, armed with sturdy weapons and a deep resolve to defend their home against the newcomers.

On the other side, the Tuatha Dé Danann were unlike any force the Fir Bolg had ever encountered. They were tall and graceful, their armor gleaming with an otherworldly light, their weapons finely crafted and enchanted with ancient magic. They were led by their king, Nuada, a wise and just leader who carried the Sword of Light, one of their four great treasures, which was said to be invincible in battle.

The two armies faced each other across the field, the tension palpable. The Fir Bolg, though outmatched in terms of magic and weaponry, were determined to fight with everything they had. The Tuatha Dé Danann, though confident in their abilities, respected their opponents' bravery and were prepared for a hard-fought battle.

The battle began with a thunderous clash as the two forces met. The Fir Bolg charged with all their might, their war cries echoing across the plains, while the Tuatha Dé Danann, with their strategic brilliance and mystical prowess, countered with a disciplined and calculated defense. The ground shook with the impact of weapons and the cries of warriors.

For days, the battle raged on. The Fir Bolg fought valiantly, refusing to yield even an inch of their land. They were led by their own king, Eochaid Mac Eirc, a formidable warrior who inspired his men with his courage and leadership. Eochaid was determined to protect his people and their way of life, even if it meant sacrificing everything.

The Tuatha Dé Danann, however, had more than just physical strength on their side. They wielded powerful magic, calling upon the elements and the forces of nature to aid them in battle. They conjured storms and fogs to confuse the enemy, summoned lightning to strike down their foes, and used illusions to deceive and disorient the Fir Bolg warriors.

One of the most fearsome warriors of the Tuatha Dé Danann was Ogma, known for his incredible strength and prowess in battle. Ogma, with his massive club, carved a path through the ranks of the Fir Bolg, his might unmatched on the battlefield. His deeds in this battle would become the stuff of legend, inspiring tales of heroism and bravery for generations to come.

Despite the overwhelming power of the Tuatha Dé Danann, the Fir Bolg fought with unmatched determination. They inflicted significant casualties on the Tuatha Dé Danann, showing that they were not to be underestimated. Their courage and tenacity earned the respect of their enemies, even as the battle turned increasingly in favor of the Tuatha Dé Danann.

On the final day of the battle, King Eochaid Mac Eirc, knowing that defeat was inevitable, made one last stand. He led his warriors into the heart of the enemy lines, determined to fight until the end. The Tuatha Dé Danann, recognizing his bravery, met his charge with a mixture of respect and sorrow, knowing that this was a warrior worthy of honor.

In the ensuing clash, Eochaid was slain by Nuada himself, the Sword of Light striking him down. With the death of their king, the Fir Bolg's resistance finally crumbled. The remaining warriors were either killed or forced to flee, and the battle came to an end.

The Tuatha Dé Danann had won the day, but the victory

came at a cost. King Nuada, in the heat of battle, had lost his hand to a fearsome Fir Bolg warrior. Though the Tuatha Dé Danann had emerged victorious, their king was now maimed, and according to their laws, a king must be whole and unblemished. This injury would have significant repercussions for the Tuatha Dé Danann, setting the stage for future conflicts and changes in leadership.

After the battle, the Tuatha Dé Danann, despite their triumph, treated the Fir Bolg with great respect. They allowed the surviving Fir Bolg to retain a portion of the land, recognizing their bravery and the honor with which they had fought. The Fir Bolg, though defeated, were not entirely vanquished, and their legacy continued in the annals of Irish myth.

The First Battle of Mag Tuired marked the beginning of the Tuatha Dé Danann's reign in Ireland. They established themselves as the rulers of the land, bringing with them their advanced knowledge, culture, and magical abilities. Their presence transformed Ireland into a land of enchantment, where the mystical and the mundane coexisted in harmony.

Yet, the story of the Tuatha Dé Danann was far from over. The loss of Nuada's hand, though seemingly a minor detail in the grand tapestry of their history, would have far-reaching consequences. The Tuatha Dé Danann were bound by their own laws and traditions, and a king who was not physically whole could not continue to rule. This dilemma would lead to the rise of a new king, Bres, whose reign would bring both challenges and strife to the Tuatha Dé Danann.

The divine race had secured their place in Ireland, but their rule would soon be tested by internal divisions and external threats, particularly from the fearsome Fomorians, a race of dark and chaotic beings with whom the Tuatha Dé Danann would have to contend in the future.

F.T. Weaver

With the victory of the Tuatha Dé Danann over the Fir Bolg, a new era began in Ireland. The Tuatha Dé Danann established their rule, bringing with them not only their martial prowess but also their wisdom, magic, and the treasures that symbolized their divine authority. King Nuada, despite losing his hand in the battle, was recognized as a fair and just ruler, beloved by his people.

However, the loss of Nuada's hand presented a significant problem. The Tuatha Dé Danann held a sacred law that a king must be physically whole and unblemished to rule. This belief was deeply ingrained in their culture, as they viewed their king as a reflection of the health and integrity of the entire land. A king with a physical imperfection was thought to bring misfortune and imbalance to the kingdom.

Nuada's injury, though grievous, had not diminished his wisdom or his leadership abilities, but the law was clear, and the Tuatha Dé Danann were bound by it. Nuada, understanding the importance of the law and the need to uphold it, knew that he could not continue to rule as king in his current state.

The Tuatha Dé Danann, faced with this dilemma, turned to their healers and craftsmen, seeking a solution that would allow Nuada to retain his throne. Among them was Dian Cecht, the god of healing, who possessed great knowledge of medicine and magic. Dian Cecht, with the help of his son Miach, set to work creating a prosthetic hand for Nuada, one made entirely of silver. This hand was not just a simple replacement—it was imbued with magical properties that allowed Nuada to use it as if it were his own flesh and bone.

The Silver Hand of Nuada, as it came to be known, was a marvel of craftsmanship and magic, a symbol of the Tuatha Dé Danann's advanced knowledge and their ability to overcome even the most challenging obstacles. With this new hand,

Nuada was once again whole, and many believed that he should be allowed to continue his reign.

However, the law remained unyielding. Despite the miraculous nature of his new hand, it was still not made of flesh, and thus, Nuada was considered no longer fit to rule. This led to a period of uncertainty and transition within the Tuatha Dé Danann.

During this time of uncertainty, a new figure emerged—Bres, the son of a Tuatha Dé Danann woman and a Fomorian prince. Bres was chosen to be the new king, partly because of his lineage, which connected him to both the Tuatha Dé Danann and the Fomorians. It was hoped that his dual heritage would bring peace and unity between the two races.

Bres was physically perfect, possessing great beauty and strength, and his selection as king was seen as a way to uphold the law while maintaining stability within the realm. However, Bres's reign would soon prove to be anything but stable.

Bres was a handsome and charismatic figure, but beneath his pleasing exterior, he lacked the qualities that had made Nuada a beloved ruler. Bres was ambitious, greedy, and devoid of the wisdom and fairness that had characterized Nuada's leadership. His Fomorian heritage also meant that he had divided loyalties, and soon, his darker nature began to surface.

Under Bres's rule, the Tuatha Dé Danann began to suffer. He imposed heavy taxes on the people, demanding tribute and labor that strained the resources of the land. He neglected the traditional duties of a king, showing little concern for the welfare of his people or the balance of the natural world. The prosperity that had flourished under Nuada's rule began to wither, and discontent grew among the

Tuatha Dé Danann.

Bres's rule also brought a more ominous change—he began to favor his Fomorian relatives, inviting them into positions of power and influence within the kingdom. The Fomorians, who were traditionally seen as a race of chaos and destruction, began to exert their influence over the land, bringing with them their harsh and oppressive ways.

The people of the Tuatha Dé Danann, who had once celebrated their victory over the Fir Bolg and looked forward to a golden age under Nuada, now found themselves oppressed and burdened under the rule of Bres. The land itself seemed to reflect the suffering of its people, as crops failed, and the once bountiful fields lay barren.

As the situation grew more dire, the dissatisfaction with Bres's rule reached a breaking point. The Tuatha Dé Danann began to remember the wisdom and fairness of Nuada's reign, and many called for his return. They longed for the days when their king had ruled with justice and compassion, guided by the principles that had always sustained their people.

Nuada, though no longer king, had not been idle during Bres's reign. He continued to lead and inspire those who remained loyal to him, offering guidance and support where he could. His prosthetic hand, though a reminder of his past injury, had not diminished his strength or his resolve.

The turning point came when Miach, the son of Dian Cecht, used his exceptional healing powers to replace Nuada's silver hand with one of flesh and bone, fully restoring Nuada to his original form. With his physical wholeness restored, there was no longer any reason to deny Nuada the throne.

The Tuatha Dé Danann, tired of Bres's misrule and yearning for the return of a just and wise leader, rallied around Nuada. Bres, seeing the tide turning against him, fled to his Fomorian kin, seeking their support to reclaim his throne by force.

This set the stage for a second and even greater conflict, the Second Battle of Mag Tuired, where the Tuatha Dé Danann would once again take up arms, this time against the Fomorians, the dark and chaotic race that had always posed a threat to the harmony of Ireland.

As the Tuatha Dé Danann prepared for this new battle, they knew that the stakes were higher than ever before. The fate of their land, their people, and their way of life hung in the balance, and the battle to come would test not only their strength and courage but also the wisdom and unity that had once defined their reign.

Nuada, restored to his former glory, would lead his people into this battle, but he would not do so alone. A new hero would emerge, one whose talents and destiny would shape the future of the Tuatha Dé Danann and the land of Ireland itself.

As the Tuatha Dé Danann prepared for the inevitable conflict with the Fomorians, a sense of urgency and foreboding swept through their ranks. They knew that this battle would not be like the first—this time, they would face an enemy whose power was fueled by chaos and destruction, a force that sought not just to conquer but to dominate and oppress.

In this time of crisis, the Tuatha Dé Danann found hope in the arrival of a new and extraordinary figure—Lugh, the son of Cian of the Tuatha Dé Danann and Ethniu, the daughter of the Fomorian leader Balor. Lugh, often referred to as Lugh of the Long Arm or Lugh Lámhfhada, was a being of immense talent and potential, known for his mastery of numerous arts and crafts.

Lugh's heritage was a unique blend of the divine and the formidable, making him a bridge between the Tuatha Dé

Danann and the Fomorians. Despite his Fomorian lineage, Lugh was fiercely loyal to the Tuatha Dé Danann, and his arrival was seen as a sign that the gods themselves had not abandoned their people.

Lugh first came to the court of Nuada, seeking to join the Tuatha Dé Danann in their struggle against the Fomorians. When he arrived at the gates of Tara, the seat of the Tuatha Dé Danann, he was initially turned away by the gatekeeper, who informed him that the court already had masters of every skill—warriors, bards, healers, craftsmen, and magicians.

But Lugh, confident in his abilities, asked, "Do you have a man who possesses all these skills in one?"

The gatekeeper was taken aback, for indeed, there was no one in the court who could claim mastery over all arts and crafts as Lugh did. Intrigued, the gatekeeper brought Lugh before King Nuada. When Lugh demonstrated his vast array of skills—warrior, poet, smith, harper, sorcerer, and healer—Nuada recognized that Lugh was no ordinary man. He was the one destined to lead the Tuatha Dé Danann to victory.

Lugh was accepted into the court with great honor, and soon, his talents became invaluable to the Tuatha Dé Danann as they prepared for the Second Battle of Mag Tuired. Lugh's leadership, strategic insight, and inspirational presence revitalized the Tuatha Dé Danann, giving them the hope and courage they needed to face the formidable Fomorian threat.

The Fomorians, led by the fearsome Balor of the Evil Eye, were a terrifying enemy. Balor was a giant with a single eye in the middle of his forehead, an eye that could unleash destruction with a mere glance. It was said that when Balor opened his eye, entire armies could be laid to waste. The Fomorians were a race of chaos and darkness, and their rule over the land would mean suffering and tyranny for all who lived under it.

As the day of the battle approached, the tension in the air was palpable. Both the Tuatha Dé Danann and the Fomorians gathered their forces on the plains of Mag Tuired, the same battlefield where the Tuatha Dé Danann had once triumphed over the Fir Bolg. But this time, the stakes were even higher.

The Tuatha Dé Danann, under the leadership of Nuada and Lugh, were prepared to fight with all their might. They knew that they faced a formidable and ruthless enemy, but they also knew that they had powerful allies and a deep connection to the land they were defending.

On the morning of the battle, the two armies clashed with a ferocity that shook the very earth. The Fomorians, with their brutish strength and dark magic, seemed unstoppable at first, pushing back the Tuatha Dé Danann with their relentless assault. The air was filled with the sounds of battle—the clash of weapons, the cries of warriors, and the roars of beasts summoned by Fomorian sorcery.

But the Tuatha Dé Danann were not easily defeated. Lugh, with his unmatched skill and tactical brilliance, led the charge, rallying his people with words of courage and hope. He fought at the forefront, his spear flashing like lightning, his sword striking down foes with deadly precision.

The battle raged on for hours, with neither side willing to give an inch. The Fomorians, led by Balor, were determined to crush the Tuatha Dé Danann and assert their dominance over the land. Balor himself was a terrifying presence on the battlefield, his eye closed but ready to unleash its deadly power at any moment.

As the battle reached its climax, Lugh faced his grandfather, Balor, in a confrontation that would decide the fate of the land. Balor, sensing that Lugh was a threat to his power, opened his eye to strike down his grandson with a single, deadly gaze. But Lugh, quick and agile, used a sling to hurl a stone directly into Balor's eye, driving it through his skull and out the back of his head. Balor, struck by his own destructive power, fell dead to the ground, his fall marking the turning point of the battle.

With Balor's death, the Fomorian forces were thrown into disarray. Leaderless and demoralized, they began to falter under the relentless assault of the Tuatha Dé Danann. Lugh, seizing the moment, led a final, decisive charge that broke the Fomorian lines and sent them fleeing from the battlefield.

The Tuatha Dé Danann had won a hard-fought and costly victory. The Second Battle of Mag Tuired was over, and the Fomorians were defeated, their dark influence driven from the land. The Tuatha Dé Danann had proven their strength, their unity, and their right to rule Ireland.

In the aftermath of the battle, King Nuada, who had fought bravely alongside his people, acknowledged the greatness of Lugh and the pivotal role he had played in securing their victory. Nuada, understanding that Lugh was the hero destined to lead them into a new age, willingly ceded his kingship to Lugh, recognizing that a new era was dawning for the Tuatha Dé Danann.

Lugh became the High King of the Tuatha Dé Danann, a leader who embodied all the virtues of his people—strength, wisdom, artistry, and a deep connection to the land. Under Lugh's rule, the Tuatha Dé Danann flourished, their culture and influence spreading across Ireland.

But even as they celebrated their victory, the Tuatha Dé Danann knew that their time as rulers of the mortal world was not eternal. The prophecies had foretold that a new race would come, one that would eventually take their place. The Tuatha Dé Danann's destiny was not to rule forever, but to lay the foundations of a land that would one day be passed on to others.

As the years passed, the Tuatha Dé Danann began to withdraw from the world of mortals, retreating into the hills, the forests, and the ancient mounds that dotted the Irish landscape. They became the Sídhe, the people of the mounds, fading into the Otherworld where they would continue to live in harmony with the land, unseen by human eyes but always present.

Their legacy, however, remained. The stories of the Tuatha Dé Danann became the foundation of Irish mythology, their deeds and their magic remembered and revered by the generations that followed. The land they had once ruled was now imbued with their spirit, and the treasures they had brought—the Stone of Fal, the Spear of Lugh, the Sword of Nuada, and the Cauldron of Dagda—became symbols of the deep connection between Ireland's people and their mythical past.

With the triumph of the Tuatha Dé Danann in the Second Battle of Mag Tuired, Ireland entered a golden age under the rule of Lugh. The land prospered, and the people thrived under the guidance of their wise and powerful leaders. The Tuatha Dé Danann brought advancements in art, science, and magic, imbuing the very essence of Ireland with their divine presence.

However, even in this time of peace and prosperity, the Tuatha Dé Danann were aware that their reign in the mortal world was not to last forever. The prophecies had long foretold the arrival of a new race, the Milesians, who would come to Ireland and eventually claim the land as their own. The Milesians were the ancestors of the Irish people, and their coming was seen as an inevitable part of the island's destiny.

The Tuatha Dé Danann, though unmatched in their power and wisdom, were not fated to rule the land indefinitely. They understood that their time as the visible rulers of Ireland was drawing to a close. This knowledge did not come with bitterness or resentment, but with a profound acceptance of the natural order of things. The Tuatha Dé Danann were beings of the Otherworld, and they knew that their true place was in the mystical realms beyond the mortal veil.

The arrival of the Milesians marked the beginning of the end for the Tuatha Dé Danann's rule. The Milesians, led by the sons of Míl Espáine, were a strong and determined people who had traveled from Iberia to claim the land that had been promised to them by their own seers and prophets. The encounter between the Tuatha Dé Danann and the Milesians was not marked by immediate conflict, but rather by a series of challenges and negotiations.

The Tuatha Dé Danann, aware of the prophecy, welcomed the Milesians and offered them hospitality, but they also set certain conditions. They proposed that the Milesians return to their ships and sail nine waves back from the shore. If they could return safely to land, the island would be theirs. The Milesians agreed, but as they sailed away, the Tuatha Dé Danann used their magic to summon a great storm, hoping to prevent the Milesians from returning.

The storm raged fiercely, and many of the Milesian ships were lost. However, the sons of Míl, led by their druid Amergin Glúingel, invoked their own magic and poetry to calm the seas and break the spell of the Tuatha Dé Danann. The Milesians returned to the shore, overcoming the challenge, and thus the prophecy was fulfilled.

Realizing that the time had come to cede the land to the new race, the Tuatha Dé Danann did not engage in a prolonged war but instead chose a different path. They withdrew from the mortal world, retreating into the hills, mountains, and ancient burial mounds known as síde. These síde became their new homes, entrances to the Otherworld where they would live in a realm parallel to the human world, invisible to most but ever-present.

The Tuatha Dé Danann's retreat to the Otherworld was not an act of defeat but one of transformation. They did not die or vanish; instead, they became the Aos Sí, the People of the Mounds, who are also known as the Sídhe or Fairy Folk. They remained guardians of the land, its secrets, and its magic, watching over Ireland from their hidden realms.

In the Otherworld, the Tuatha Dé Danann continued to thrive, their lives timeless and their powers undiminished. They became part of the land itself, intertwined with the natural world in a way that few mortals could understand. The places where they once ruled became sacred sites, imbued with the lingering presence of their magic. Hills, rivers, and ancient sites across Ireland were named after them, and these places became the focus of worship and reverence in the centuries that followed.

Though the Tuatha Dé Danann no longer walked openly among mortals, their influence persisted in the culture and folklore of Ireland. The stories of their deeds, their battles, and their wisdom were passed down through generations, becoming an integral part of Irish identity and heritage. The Tuatha Dé Danann were remembered not only as rulers and warriors but also as teachers, healers, and bringers of knowledge.

The legacy of the Tuatha Dé Danann is reflected in the many tales of the Irish Otherworld, a realm that exists alongside the mortal world, accessible only to those with the right knowledge or through certain mystical events. The Otherworld is a place of eternal youth, beauty, and abundance, where the Tuatha Dé Danann continue to hold court, feasting and reveling in their timeless existence.

F.T. Weaver

The Cultural Significance and Other Cultural Facts About "The Tuatha Dé Danann"

The Tuatha Dé Danann are one of the most significant and enigmatic groups in Irish mythology, embodying the mysticism, spirituality, and cultural values of ancient Ireland. Their story, which includes their arrival, reign, and eventual retreat into the Otherworld, is rich with symbolic meaning and has had a lasting impact on Irish culture, folklore, and identity. Understanding the cultural significance of the Tuatha Dé Danann requires an exploration of their role in Irish mythology, their symbolic representations, and their enduring influence on Irish literature, art, and national consciousness.

The Tuatha Dé Danann in Irish Mythology

Origins and Arrival

The Tuatha Dé Danann, often translated as "the People of the Goddess Danu," are depicted as a divine race of beings with extraordinary powers, knowledge, and beauty. According to myth, they came to Ireland from distant, mystical lands, bringing with them the knowledge of magic, arts, and science. Their arrival in Ireland is marked by mystery and wonder, often described as descending from the skies in dark clouds or arriving by sea and burning their ships to ensure they could never leave.

The Tuatha Dé Danann's origins are linked to the goddess Danu, considered the mother of the gods and a personification of the earth and fertility. This connection to Danu ties the Tuatha Dé Danann to the natural world and emphasizes their role as guardians of the land and its mysteries. Their arrival in Ireland is not just a physical migration but a symbolic establishment of a new order, one that blends the mystical with the earthly.

Symbolic Treasures

The Tuatha Dé Danann brought with them four great treasures, each imbued with powerful symbolism:

The Stone of Fal (Lia Fáil): A sacred stone that would cry out when the rightful king of Ireland touched it. It symbolizes the divine right to rule and the connection between the king and the land.

The Spear of Lugh: A weapon that never missed its mark and assured victory. It represents martial prowess and the inevitability of fate.

The Sword of Nuada (Claíomh Solais): A sword of light that was unstoppable in battle. This treasure symbolizes justice, authority, and the protection of the community.

The Cauldron of Dagda: A cauldron that provided endless sustenance, ensuring that no one who approached it would leave hungry. It represents abundance, hospitality, and the nurturing aspect of leadership.

These treasures are not only magical artifacts but also embodiments of the qualities that the Tuatha Dé Danann brought to Ireland—sovereignty, protection, justice, and abundance. They reflect the values that were central to the Tuatha Dé Danann's rule and are symbolic of the ideal relationship between rulers and their land.

Battles and Sovereignty

The story of the Tuatha Dé Danann is also one of conflict and the struggle for sovereignty. Their battles, particularly the First and Second Battles of Mag Tuired, are central to their mythological narrative. These battles are not just physical confrontations but symbolic struggles between different forces—light and darkness, order and chaos, civilization and barbarism.

In the First Battle of Mag Tuired, the Tuatha Dé Danann fought against the Fir Bolg, the previous inhabitants of Ireland. This battle represents the establishment of a new order, with the

Tuatha Dé Danann bringing their superior knowledge and magic to the land. Their victory over the Fir Bolg symbolizes the triumph of a more advanced civilization and the beginning of their golden age.

The Second Battle of Mag Tuired is fought against the Fomorians, a race often depicted as monstrous and chaotic beings. The Fomorians represent the destructive and chaotic forces in the world, and the battle against them symbolizes the struggle to maintain order and justice. Lugh's defeat of Balor, the Fomorian leader, is a pivotal moment that signifies the victory of light over darkness and the protection of the land from malevolent forces.

These battles also reflect the cyclical nature of power and the inevitability of change. While the Tuatha Dé Danann are victorious, their time as rulers is not eternal. Their eventual retreat into the Otherworld marks the end of their dominance in the mortal realm, making way for the next race, the Milesians, who are the ancestors of the Irish people.

The Retreat to the Otherworld

The Sidhe and the Otherworld

The Tuatha Dé Danann's retreat into the Otherworld is one of the most intriguing aspects of their story. After the arrival of the Milesians, the Tuatha Dé Danann did not disappear but instead retreated into the hills, mounds, and other ancient sites across Ireland. These places, known as síde (singular síd), became their new homes, and the Tuatha Dé Danann became known as the Aos Sí or the Sídhe—the fairy folk or the people of the mounds.

The Otherworld in Irish mythology is a parallel realm, a place of eternal youth, beauty, and abundance, where time flows differently from the mortal world. The Tuatha Dé Danann's transition to the Otherworld represents their transformation from earthly rulers to guardians of the land's spiritual essence. They continue to exist, but in a different form, watching over Ireland and occasionally interacting with the mortal world.

This retreat is not an act of defeat but one of preservation and transformation. The Tuatha Dé Danann become part of the landscape itself, their presence woven into the very fabric of Ireland's natural and cultural heritage. They are seen as protectors of the land, and their connection to the Otherworld reflects the Irish belief in the thin veil between the physical and spiritual realms.

Influence on Folklore and Tradition

The Tuatha Dé Danann's retreat into the Otherworld has had a profound impact on Irish folklore and tradition. They are often depicted as the fairy folk or the Daoine Sidhe, beings who possess great power and must be treated with respect. The Irish landscape is filled with places associated with the Tuatha Dé Danann, and many traditions and customs are rooted in the belief that they still inhabit these sacred sites.

For example, fairy forts, ringforts, and certain natural features like hills, rivers, and trees are often associated with the Tuatha Dé Danann. These places are considered to be entrances to the Otherworld, and it is believed that disturbing them can bring misfortune. This belief has influenced land use and preservation practices in Ireland, where there is a deep respect for these ancient sites.

The Tuatha Dé Danann also feature prominently in seasonal festivals such as Samhain and Beltane, which mark the transitions between seasons and the movement of the Tuatha Dé Danann between the worlds. These festivals celebrate the connection between the human and the divine, the natural and the supernatural, and they honor the Tuatha Dé Danann as the guardians of these transitions.

F.T. Weaver

Cultural and Literary Impact

Influence on Irish Literature

The Tuatha Dé Danann have had a significant influence on Irish literature, particularly during the Irish Literary Revival of the late 19th and early 20th centuries. Writers like W.B. Yeats, Lady Gregory, and James Stephens drew heavily on the mythology of the Tuatha Dé Danann in their works, using these ancient stories to explore themes of national identity, spirituality, and the connection between Ireland's past and present.

Yeats, in particular, was fascinated by the Tuatha Dé Danann and the Otherworld. In his poetry and plays, he often depicted the Tuatha Dé Danann as symbols of Ireland's lost golden age, a time of harmony between the human and the divine. Yeats's work contributed to the revival of interest in Irish mythology and helped to solidify the Tuatha Dé Danann's place in the national consciousness.

The Tuatha Dé Danann also appear in modern fantasy literature, where they are often depicted as powerful, otherworldly beings who influence the course of events in the mortal world. Their story has inspired countless writers and continues to captivate audiences with its blend of magic, heroism, and mystery.

The Tuatha Dé Danann and National Identity

The Tuatha Dé Danann have become symbols of Irish cultural identity, representing the mystical and spiritual aspects of the land and its people. Their story is often invoked in discussions of Ireland's ancient heritage and the deep connection between the Irish people and their natural environment.

The idea of the Tuatha Dé Danann as the original inhabitants of Ireland, who retreated into the Otherworld to make way for the mortal races, reflects the theme of continuity and preservation. They are seen as the keepers of Ireland's ancient knowledge and traditions, and their legacy is a reminder of the enduring power of myth and the importance of preserving cultural heritage.

The Tuatha Dé Danann's role as protectors of the land also resonates with modern environmental movements in Ireland, where there is a strong emphasis on the preservation of natural landscapes and the recognition of the land's sacredness. The Tuatha Dé Danann, as beings who embody the spirit of the land, are seen as symbols of this environmental consciousness.

The Symbolism of the Tuatha Dé Danann

Guardians of Knowledge and Culture
The Tuatha Dé Danann are often depicted as the bringers and protectors of knowledge, culture, and the arts. Their mastery of magic, healing, and craftsmanship symbolizes the importance of wisdom and creativity in society. They are the archetypal guardians of the cultural and spiritual heritage of Ireland, ensuring that the knowledge of the past is not lost but passed down through the generations.

Their four great treasures are not just powerful artifacts but also symbols of the values they brought to Ireland—justice, protection, abundance, and the rightful rule. These treasures represent the ideal qualities of leadership and the responsibilities that come with power.

The Tuatha Dé Danann's role as guardians of knowledge is also reflected in their connection to the druids, the learned class of ancient Celtic society. The druids were the keepers of sacred knowledge, and the Tuatha Dé Danann, as divine beings, are often seen as their patrons and teachers.

The Cycle of Power and the Acceptance of Change
The story of the Tuatha Dé Danann also reflects the cyclical nature of power and the inevitability of change. Their arrival in

Ireland marks the beginning of a new era, but their eventual retreat into the Otherworld signifies the natural progression of time and the passing of the torch to a new race. This cycle of rise and fall is a common theme in mythology and reflects the understanding that all things are transient and that change is a fundamental part of life.

The Tuatha Dé Danann's acceptance of their fate and their graceful retreat into the Otherworld highlight the importance of adaptability and the ability to embrace change. Rather than fighting against their destiny, they chose to transform and continue their existence in a different form. This adaptability is a key aspect of their wisdom and is a lesson that resonates with the human experience.

Conclusion

The Tuatha Dé Danann are more than just mythological figures; they are central to the cultural and spiritual heritage of Ireland. Their story is a complex and multifaceted narrative that encompasses themes of sovereignty, wisdom, transformation, and the connection between the human and the divine. Through their battles, their treasures, and their eventual retreat into the Otherworld, the Tuatha Dé Danann have left an indelible mark on Irish culture and identity.

Their legacy continues to inspire and influence, not only in folklore and literature but also in the way the Irish people relate to their land and their past. The Tuatha Dé Danann are symbols of the enduring power of myth, the importance of cultural preservation, and the deep spiritual connection between Ireland and its people. Their story is a testament to the richness of Irish mythology and the timelessness of the lessons it imparts.

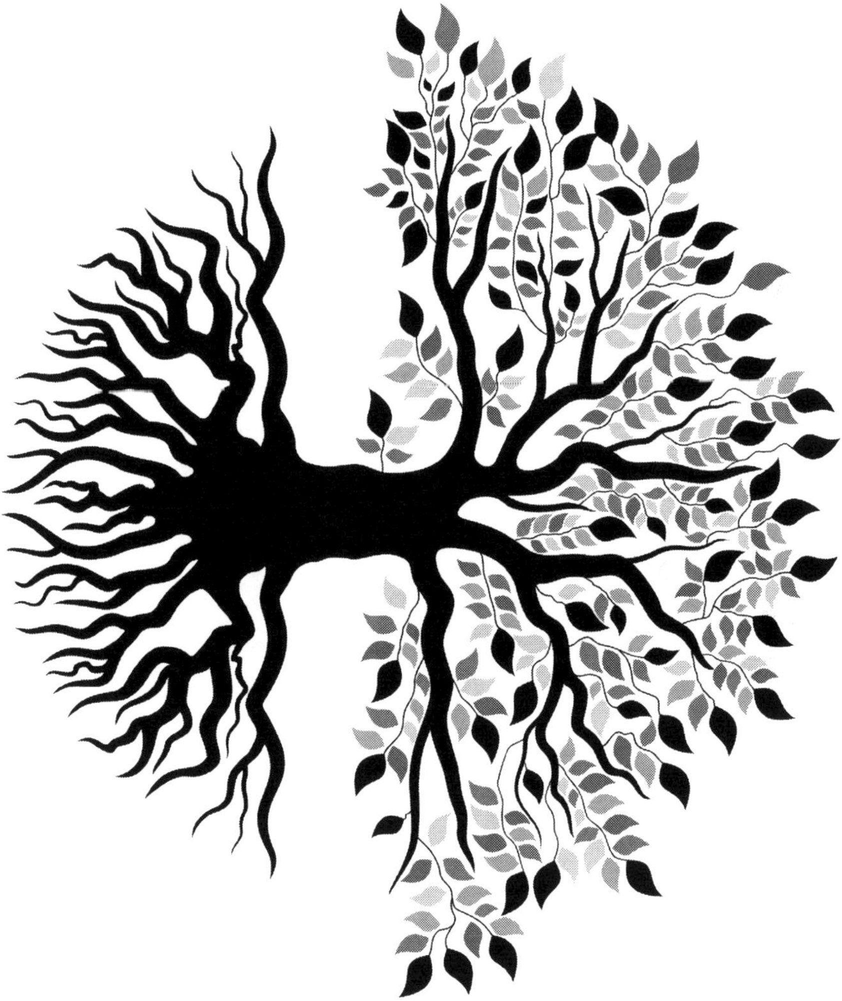

The Tale of Deirdre of the Sorrows

In the ancient kingdom of Ulster, during a time when heroes walked the earth and the gods still spoke through the lips of seers, a prophecy was uttered that would set the course for one of the most tragic tales in Irish mythology—the story of Deirdre of the Sorrows.

It began one fateful evening in the great hall of King Conchobar mac Nessa, the ruler of Ulster. The king was holding a feast for his nobles and warriors when Cathbad, the chief druid and seer of the court, was struck by a powerful vision. The room fell silent as Cathbad's eyes glazed over, his voice deep and resonant as he spoke of a child yet unborn.

"A child will be born," he said, "a girl of such beauty that she will bring ruin upon the greatest men of Ulster. Her beauty will cause strife, bloodshed, and sorrow, and her name will be remembered through the ages as Deirdre of the Sorrows."

The prophecy sent a chill through the hall, and King Conchobar, though troubled by the druid's words, was also intrigued. He was a man of ambition and desire, and the thought of a woman whose beauty could rival the sun and the moon filled him with both dread and fascination.

Some time later, in the household of Fedlimid, the royal storyteller, a child was born—a girl of extraordinary beauty, even in infancy. She was named Deirdre, and from the moment of her birth, it was clear that she was no ordinary child. Her eyes shone with an ethereal light, and her skin was as fair as the first snow of winter.

But Deirdre's birth was not celebrated with joy, for the prophecy of Cathbad weighed heavily on the minds of those who knew of it. To prevent the doom foretold by the druid, King Conchobar decided that Deirdre would be taken from her family and raised in seclusion, far from the eyes of men. He decreed that she would be kept safe and untouched until she was of age, at which time she would become his queen.

And so, Deirdre was taken to a remote and secretive place, a fortress deep in the woods, where she was cared for by her nurse, Lavarcam, who was both wise and kind. Lavarcam raised Deirdre with love, teaching her the arts of music, poetry, and weaving, and ensuring that she grew up with a gentle heart and a sharp mind.

Deirdre's beauty blossomed as she grew, and Lavarcam, who had seen much of the world, often marveled at the child's radiance. Yet, despite the idyllic surroundings and the care she received, Deirdre was not content. She often felt a deep, inexplicable sadness, a longing for something beyond the walls of her seclusion.

As the years passed, Deirdre became curious about the world outside her fortress. She would ask Lavarcam about the land of Ulster, its people, and the great warriors who served King Conchobar. Lavarcam, bound by her duty, tried to keep Deirdre's curiosity in check, but she could not deny the girl her natural yearning to know more.

One winter's day, as the snow lay thick on the ground,

F.T. Weaver

Deirdre looked out of her window and saw a raven pecking at the carcass of a lamb in the snow. The sight of the black raven against the white snow, stained with the red blood of the lamb, struck Deirdre with a strange vision of beauty.

She turned to Lavarcam and said, "I dream of a man with hair as black as the raven, skin as white as the snow, and lips as red as the blood."

Lavarcam, troubled by Deirdre's words, knew that the time had come when the prophecy would begin to unfold. The description that Deirdre had unknowingly given was that of Naoise, a young warrior of the Red Branch, one of the most handsome and noble men in all of Ulster.

Lavarcam, fearing for Deirdre's fate, tried to dissuade her from thoughts of such a man, but it was too late. The image had taken root in Deirdre's heart, and her thoughts turned more and more to the world beyond her secluded life.

As Deirdre grew older, her beauty became the stuff of legend. Though she had never been seen by the people of Ulster, stories of her loveliness spread far and wide, stoking the fires of curiosity and desire in the hearts of many. Yet, none dared approach her, for they knew that she was destined for King Conchobar, and the prophecy of her bringing sorrow was still remembered.

But fate, as it often does, had other plans. Deirdre's life, which had been so carefully guarded and controlled, was about to change forever with the arrival of Naoise, the man of her visions and the one who would set in motion the tragic events foretold by Cathbad.

As Deirdre approached womanhood, the day came when the threads of fate began to weave together, leading her towards the destiny that had been foretold. Despite the seclusion in which she had been kept, her beauty and the prophecy of her future had spread across Ulster, and whispers of the girl destined to be King Conchobar's queen reached the ears of many.

It was during this time that Naoise, a warrior of the Red Branch and a member of the Clan Uisneach, was hunting in the woods near Deirdre's secluded home. Naoise was known throughout Ulster for his remarkable handsomeness, bravery, and noble spirit. His hair was as black as the raven's wing, his skin as fair as the snow, and his lips as red as blood—just as Deirdre had envisioned.

While hunting, Naoise stopped to rest and began to sing. His voice, rich and melodious, carried through the forest, reaching Deirdre's ears. The sound captivated her, filling her heart with a longing she had never felt before. She had heard many tales of the warriors of Ulster, but none had affected her as deeply as the voice of this unknown singer.

Unable to resist, Deirdre persuaded Lavarcam to bring the singer to her. Lavarcam, fearing the consequences, tried to dissuade Deirdre, but the young woman's determination was unwavering. Reluctantly, Lavarcam sent word to Naoise, inviting him to the fortress under the pretense of offering hospitality to a wandering traveler.

When Naoise arrived, he was struck by Deirdre's beauty, which surpassed all the tales he had heard. Her presence was like the dawn breaking over the hills, radiant and full of promise. Deirdre, in turn, felt an immediate and deep connection to Naoise, recognizing in him the man of her dreams.

Their meeting was brief, but the bond that formed between them was instant and unbreakable. Deirdre, seeing the future she dreaded if she were to marry King Conchobar, begged Naoise to take her away. She knew that their love was forbidden and that they were risking everything, but the thought of living without him was unbearable.

Naoise, though aware of the dangers, was equally unable to resist the pull of their mutual love. He knew that defying King Conchobar would make them outlaws, hunted and pursued by the might of Ulster, but his heart was now entwined with Deirdre's, and he could not turn away from her plea.

With a heavy heart, but resolute in their decision, Naoise agreed to flee with Deirdre. They were joined by Naoise's brothers, Ardan and Ainnle, who were also warriors of great skill and loyalty. Together, they made a pact to protect Deirdre at all costs, vowing to keep her safe from any harm that might come their way.

The four of them—Deirdre, Naoise, Ardan, and Ainnle—left the secluded fortress under the cover of night, embarking on a journey into the wilderness. They traveled across the land, moving from place to place, always staying one step ahead of the forces that Conchobar had sent to track them down.

For a time, they found refuge in the remote and wild places of Ireland, living in forests and caves, away from the reach of the king. Despite the hardships of their life on the run, Deirdre and Naoise's love only grew stronger, and the bonds between them and Naoise's brothers deepened. They lived like exiles, but their love and loyalty to each other made their existence bearable.

Yet, the shadow of King Conchobar's wrath loomed large over them. Conchobar, upon discovering Deirdre's flight with Naoise, was consumed with anger and jealousy. The woman he had claimed for himself had been taken by another, and his pride and authority had been challenged. He swore that he would not rest until Deirdre was returned to him and Naoise and his brothers were punished.

The king's pursuit was relentless, and though the lovers and their companions managed to evade capture for a time, they knew that they could not remain in Ireland forever. The constant threat of discovery and the harsh conditions of their life on the run took a toll on them, and they began to consider leaving the island altogether.

Eventually, they decided to cross the sea to Scotland, seeking refuge among the distant isles where they hoped to find peace and safety far from Conchobar's reach. In Scotland, they found sanctuary among the Picts, a people known for their independence and warrior spirit. The Pictish king welcomed them and offered them protection, moved by their plight and impressed by the honor and courage of the brothers.

For a time, Deirdre and Naoise lived in relative peace, surrounded by the rugged beauty of the Scottish landscape. They built a life together, and though they missed their homeland, they were grateful for the reprieve from the constant fear of pursuit. Deirdre, in particular, flourished in this new land, her spirit brightening in the company of Naoise and his brothers.

However, the peace they found in Scotland was not to last. Back in Ulster, King Conchobar's anger had not abated. He could not forget the slight to his pride or the loss of Deirdre, whose beauty had become an obsession. Determined to bring her back to Ulster and exact his revenge on Naoise and his brothers, Conchobar devised a cunning plan.

He sent messengers to the Pictish king, bearing gifts and words of friendship. In these messages, Conchobar swore that all was forgiven and that he longed for Deirdre and the sons of Uisneach to return home, promising them safety and pardon. The Pictish king, believing Conchobar's promises, urged Deirdre and Naoise to return to Ireland, thinking that it would bring an end to their life of exile.

Naoise and his brothers were wary, suspecting treachery,

but Deirdre, though fearful, was swayed by the hope of returning to the land she loved. She longed to see the green hills of Ireland again, to walk its forests and breathe its air. Reluctantly, they agreed to return, placing their trust in the word of the Pictish king and the hope that Conchobar's anger had cooled.

With heavy hearts and a sense of foreboding, they set sail for Ireland, unaware of the fate that awaited them upon their return.

The journey back to Ireland was filled with a mixture of hope and dread. Deirdre, Naoise, and his brothers, Ardan and Ainnle, had enjoyed a brief period of peace in Scotland, but the prospect of returning to their homeland tugged at their hearts. Despite their fears, they were lured by the promise of safety and a desire to see their beloved Ulster once more.

As their ship approached the shores of Ireland, Deirdre felt a sense of unease. The once familiar coastline seemed shadowed by an impending doom, and the songs of the seabirds overhead sounded more like mournful cries than joyful calls. Her heart was heavy, and she could not shake the feeling that their return would bring only sorrow.

Upon landing, they were met by Conchobar's messengers, who greeted them with false smiles and words of welcome. The messengers conveyed Conchobar's assurance that he had forgiven them and that they were to be honored guests at his court. Despite their reservations, the brothers decided to trust in the king's words, hoping that the years of exile had softened his heart.

The group made their way to Emain Macha, the royal seat of Ulster, where Conchobar awaited their arrival. As they traveled through the familiar lands of their youth, memories of happier times surfaced, and for a moment, they allowed themselves to believe that peace was possible.

However, Deirdre's intuition continued to trouble her. She had dreamt of dark omens, and her unease only grew stronger as they neared the king's fortress. She tried to voice her concerns to Naoise, but he, ever the brave and honorable warrior, reassured her that they had done nothing to warrant Conchobar's wrath and that the king's promise of safety must be genuine.

As they arrived at Emain Macha, the gates opened to welcome them, and they were led into the grand hall where Conchobar sat upon his throne. The king's eyes gleamed with a cold, calculating light as he watched Deirdre and the sons of Uisneach enter. His face was a mask of courtesy, but underneath, his heart burned with jealousy and vengeance.

Conchobar greeted them warmly, offering them seats of honor and feasting them with the best food and drink the court had to offer. Yet, beneath the veneer of hospitality, there was a tension in the air, a sense that all was not as it seemed. The warriors of the Red Branch, who had once been Naoise's comrades, now looked upon him with suspicion and unease.

As the night wore on, Conchobar's true intentions began to reveal themselves. He had no intention of honoring his promises of peace and safety. Instead, he had planned a treacherous trap, using the pretense of reconciliation to lure Naoise and his brothers back to Ulster, where he could exact his revenge.

Conchobar ordered the brothers to be separated, each taken to different parts of the fortress under the guise of showing them the accommodations prepared for their stay. Deirdre, sensing the imminent danger, tried to stay close to Naoise, but they were forcibly parted, her protests falling on deaf ears.

In the dead of night, Conchobar's men, led by the treacherous Eoghan Mac Durthacht, fell upon the sons of

Uisneach while they slept, armed with orders to kill. Despite their valor and skill, Naoise, Ardan, and Ainnle were overwhelmed by the sheer number of attackers. The brothers fought bravely, but they were no match for the king's men, who struck them down without mercy.

Deirdre's worst fears were realized when she was awakened by the sounds of the struggle and the cries of the dying. She rushed to find Naoise, but it was too late. She found him lying on the cold stone floor, his life slipping away, his blood staining the ground where they had once hoped to find peace.

Kneeling beside Naoise, Deirdre's heart shattered. She cradled his head in her lap, her tears falling like rain upon his face. The light in his eyes dimmed as he spoke his final words to her, a whisper of love that echoed through the emptiness that would follow.

The king's men, having completed their bloody task, seized Deirdre and brought her before Conchobar. The king looked upon her with a twisted satisfaction, believing that he had finally won. Deirdre, however, was beyond the reach of his control. Her spirit was broken, but her love for Naoise had given her a strength that Conchobar could not comprehend.

She stood before the king, her eyes filled with a mixture of sorrow and defiance. Conchobar, expecting her to submit to his will now that her beloved was dead, was met instead with her unwavering rejection. She refused to be his queen, refusing to bow to the man who had orchestrated the death of the only one she had ever loved.

Enraged by her defiance, Conchobar ordered that Deirdre be imprisoned, thinking that time and solitude would break her spirit. He could not understand that her love for Naoise was stronger than any chains he could place upon her. Deirdre, now alone and consumed by grief, withdrew into herself, her once radiant beauty now a reflection of her sorrow.

For a year, Deirdre was held captive, her days filled with nothing but memories of Naoise and the brothers who had died for her. Her beauty, which had once been a source of pride and envy, became a curse, reminding her of the prophecy that had foretold her tragic fate.

Conchobar, still hoping to claim her as his queen, was persistent in his advances, but Deirdre remained resolute in her rejection. She could not be swayed by his promises of power or comfort. Her heart was with Naoise, and she longed only to be reunited with him in death.

In the end, Deirdre's sorrow consumed her. Unable to bear the thought of living without Naoise and unwilling to submit to Conchobar, she took her own life, her final act of defiance against the king who had brought so much suffering to her and those she loved.

It is said that as she died, she whispered Naoise's name, her soul finding peace as it left the mortal world to join him in the afterlife. Deirdre's death was a tragedy that shook all of Ulster, and her story became a warning of the destructive power of jealousy and the consequences of defying fate.

In the years that followed, Deirdre of the Sorrows became a figure of legend, her story told and retold around the fires of Ireland. She was remembered not only for her beauty but for the love that had defied a king and for the sorrow that had ultimately claimed her life. Her tale became a part of the rich tapestry of Irish mythology, a reminder of the complexities of love, fate, and the human heart.

Cultural Significance and Other Cultural Facts About "Deirdre of the Sorrows"

"Deirdre of the Sorrows," also known as "Deirdre and the Sons of Uisneach," is one of the most enduring and poignant tales from the Ulster Cycle of Irish mythology. It is a story that has captivated audiences for centuries with its themes of love, beauty, jealousy, betrayal, and tragedy. The tale is deeply woven into the cultural fabric of Ireland, reflecting both the values and the complexities of human emotions that have been central to Irish storytelling.

The Ulster Cycle and Its Place in Irish Mythology

The Ulster Cycle, one of the four great cycles of Irish mythology, is a collection of heroic legends and sagas centered around the warriors of Ulster, particularly the Red Branch Knights, and their interactions with other kingdoms and supernatural beings. These stories are set in a time of legendary heroes and kings, a period that combines historical elements with mythological themes. The Ulster Cycle is also known for its exploration of human passions, conflicts, and the often tragic consequences of pride and honor.

"Deirdre of the Sorrows" is one of the most famous tales from this cycle and stands out for its focus on a female protagonist, a rarity in the male-dominated world of ancient heroic narratives. The story's emphasis on Deirdre's experiences, emotions, and choices highlights the importance of individual agency and the impact of personal decisions on the wider community, making it a tale of both personal and collective tragedy.

Symbolism of Deirdre and Her Beauty

Deirdre herself is a symbol of beauty and its double-edged nature in mythology. Her extraordinary beauty is both a blessing and a curse, a source of joy and destruction. From the moment of her birth, Deirdre's beauty is prophesied to bring about great sorrow, setting the stage for the inevitable tragedy that unfolds. This motif of beauty leading to downfall is common in many cultures, but in the Irish context, it is imbued with a deep sense of fatalism.

Deirdre's beauty also represents the natural world and its untamed, unpredictable power. In many ways, she is a personification of Ireland itself—beautiful, wild, and coveted, yet also vulnerable to the destructive desires of those who seek to possess it. Her life story, therefore, can be seen as an allegory for the struggles and sufferings of Ireland, caught between powerful forces beyond its control.

Themes of Love and Tragedy

The love story between Deirdre and Naoise is central to the tale and serves as a powerful narrative about the nature of love, loyalty, and the consequences of defying societal expectations. Their love is pure and intense, but it exists in a world where political power and personal desires are often at odds with one another. The decision to flee with Naoise, made out of love and a desire for freedom, ultimately leads to their downfall, reflecting the tragic inevitability that permeates much of Irish mythology.

The tragic dimension of the story is amplified by the actions of King Conchobar, whose jealousy and pride set the tragic events in motion. Conchobar's inability to accept Deirdre's love for another man and his determination to possess her at any cost highlight the destructive power of unchecked desire and the moral consequences of betrayal and revenge. The story critiques the abuse of power and the moral failings of leadership, themes that resonate strongly in Irish culture.

The Role of Prophecy and Fate

Prophecy plays a crucial role in "Deirdre of the Sorrows," as it does in many Irish myths. The prophecy made by Cathbad the druid about Deirdre's beauty and its consequences casts a shadow over her entire life, shaping the decisions of those around her and creating a sense of inescapable destiny. This element of fate underscores the tragic nature of the story, as the characters struggle against a future that seems predetermined.

The presence of prophecy in the tale reflects the Irish belief in the power of fate and the influence of the supernatural on human lives. It suggests that while humans have agency and make choices, they are also subject to forces beyond their control—forces that can lead to unexpected and often tragic outcomes. This tension between free will and destiny is a recurring theme in Irish mythology and is one of the elements that give "Deirdre of the Sorrows" its enduring emotional power.

The Cultural Impact of the Story

"Deirdre of the Sorrows" has had a significant impact on Irish culture, both in its original mythological context and in its later adaptations and reinterpretations. The story has been a source of inspiration for poets, playwrights, and writers throughout the centuries, and its themes of love, tragedy, and fate have resonated with audiences in different eras.

In the Irish Literary Revival of the late 19th and early 20th centuries, the story of Deirdre was revisited and reimagined by several prominent figures, including W.B. Yeats and John Millington Synge. These writers were drawn to the story's emotional depth and its exploration of universal themes, using it to express the complexities of Irish identity, history, and the human condition.

Synge's play "Deirdre of the Sorrows," written in 1909, is one of the most famous adaptations of the tale. Although it was *unfinished at the time of Synge's death, the play captures the essence of the myth while also infusing it with the playwright's own perspective on the tragic beauty of life and the inevitability of suffering. Synge's adaptation, along with others from the same period, helped to cement Deirdre's place as a symbol of Ireland's cultural and literary heritage.*

The story has also been interpreted as an allegory for Ireland's political struggles, particularly in the context of British rule and the quest for Irish independence. Deirdre's captivity and the conflict between love and power can be seen as reflecting the larger narrative of Ireland's fight for freedom and the personal sacrifices that such a struggle entails.

The Role of Women in Irish Mythology

Deirdre is one of the most prominent female figures in Irish mythology, and her story provides valuable insight into the role of women in these ancient narratives. While many myths focus on male heroes and their exploits, the story of Deirdre centers on a woman's experience, her emotions, and her agency. This focus on a female protagonist is significant in a mythological tradition where women's roles are often secondary or symbolic.

Deirdre's character embodies both strength and vulnerability, and her actions are driven by love, loyalty, and a desire for autonomy. Her story highlights the limited options available to women in a patriarchal society, where their beauty and desirability can become both a source of power and a cause of their downfall. Despite these limitations, Deirdre's determination to live on her terms, even in the face of overwhelming odds, makes her a powerful and enduring figure in Irish mythology.

The tale also reflects the complex portrayal of women in Irish myth, where female characters are often multifaceted, embodying a range of qualities from nurturing to warrior-like.

Deirdre's beauty is central to the story, but it is her inner strength, her love for Naoise, and her refusal to submit to Conchobar's will that define her character and make her story so compelling.

The Enduring Legacy of "Deirdre of the Sorrows"

The tale of Deirdre of the Sorrows continues to captivate audiences today, not only in Ireland but around the world. Its exploration of timeless themes—love and loss, beauty and envy, fate and free will—gives it a universal appeal, while its roots in Irish culture and history make it a vital part of the country's literary and mythological heritage.

The story's influence can be seen in various forms of art, including literature, drama, music, and visual art. It has inspired countless adaptations, retellings, and interpretations, each adding new layers of meaning to the original myth. This ability to inspire and adapt is a testament to the story's depth and the resonance of its themes.

In contemporary culture, Deirdre's story is often used to explore issues of identity, power, and the consequences of desire. It is a story that challenges readers and audiences to reflect on the complexities of human relationships and the ways in which love, beauty, and fate can shape our lives in profound and sometimes tragic ways.

Conclusion

"Deirdre of the Sorrows" is more than just a tale of tragic love; it is a story that delves deep into the human condition, exploring the interplay of emotions, desires, and fate in a way that is both timeless and uniquely Irish. Its cultural significance lies not only in its place within the Ulster Cycle but also in its *enduring impact on Irish literature, art, and identity.*

Through the character of Deirdre, the story offers a poignant reflection on the power of beauty and love, the inevitability of sorrow, and the tension between individual desires and societal expectations. It is a story that speaks to the heart, evoking empathy and reflection, and reminding us of the enduring power of myth to illuminate the truths of the human experience.

The legacy of "Deirdre of the Sorrows" continues to thrive, ensuring that the tale, like Deirdre herself, will be remembered for generations to come, a symbol of the beauty and tragedy that define the human spirit.

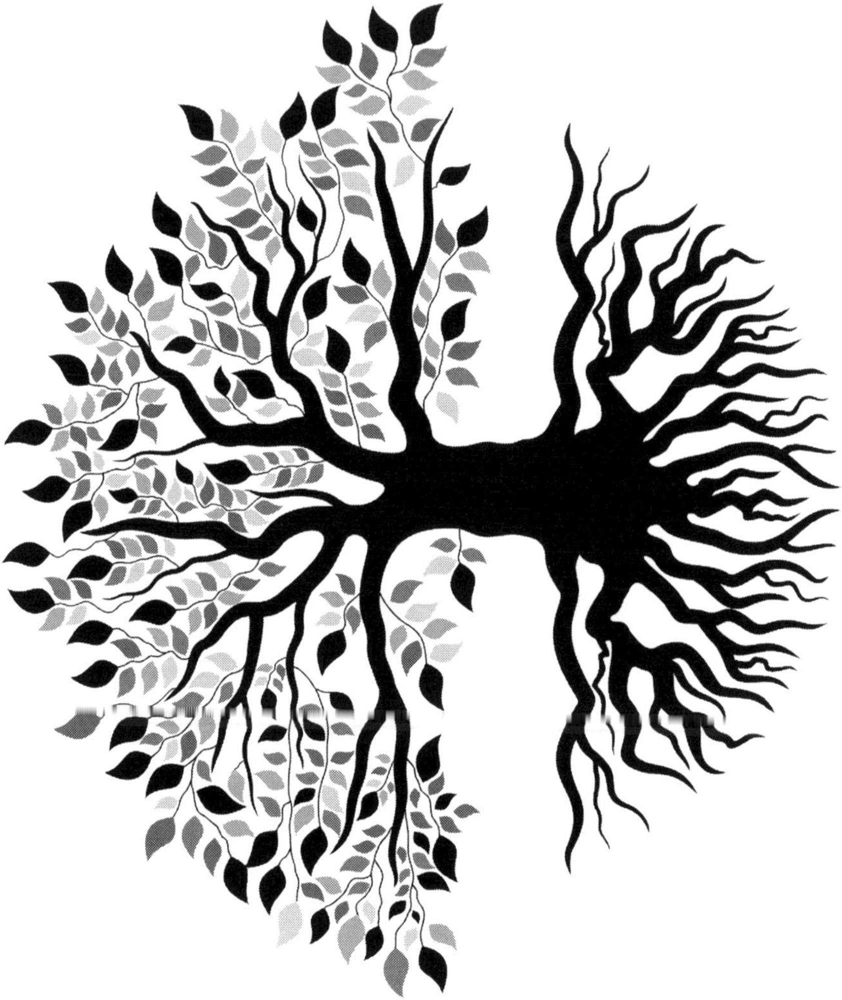

The Tale of The Battle of the Trees (Cad Goddeu)

In the ancient and enchanted lands of Wales, where the veil between the mortal world and the mystical realms was thin, there lived a powerful magician named Gwydion. Gwydion was not just any magician; he was a master of transformation, a weaver of spells, and a keeper of ancient knowledge passed down through the ages. His wisdom was unparalleled, and his connection to the natural world ran deep, as if he were in tune with the very heartbeat of the earth.

The world in which Gwydion lived was one where gods, spirits, and magical creatures roamed freely, their actions shaping the fate of both the seen and unseen worlds. Among these powerful beings was Arawn, the Lord of Annwn, the Otherworld. Annwn was a realm shrouded in mystery and shadow, a place where the spirits of the dead dwelled, and where the rules of the mortal world did not apply. Arawn, with his dark, enigmatic presence, ruled over this realm with a cunning and ambition that few could match.

The story begins with a great act of treachery: the theft of the Cauldron of Inspiration. This cauldron was a sacred object, filled with the Awen—the flowing spirit of inspiration, wisdom, and poetic creativity. It was a treasure of the gods, a source of power and enlightenment, and its presence ensured the balance between the worlds. The cauldron was closely guarded by the goddess Ceridwen, a figure of transformation and prophecy, who used it to brew the elixir of knowledge.

But Arawn, ever ambitious and desiring to extend his dominion, had managed to steal the cauldron and take it to Annwn. With the cauldron in his possession, Arawn held the power to control the flow of inspiration and knowledge, tipping the balance of power in his favor. This act was not just an affront to the gods but a threat to the natural order of the world.

Gwydion, sensing the disturbance caused by the cauldron's absence, knew that something had to be done. He understood the importance of the cauldron—it was not merely a vessel of power, but a symbol of the divine connection between the gods and the natural world. Without it, the flow of Awen would be disrupted, and both the mortal and supernatural realms would suffer.

Determined to restore balance and reclaim the cauldron, Gwydion set his mind to a plan that would require all his magical prowess. He knew that confronting Arawn directly in the shadowy depths of Annwn would be a perilous task, for Arawn's power in his own realm was nearly absolute. Gwydion needed an army, but not one of mere mortals; he needed an army that could withstand the terrors of the Otherworld and face the dark forces of Annwn.

It was then that Gwydion conceived a plan as audacious as it was ingenious. He would summon the very trees and plants of the earth to fight for him. The ancient forests of Wales were filled with trees that had stood for centuries, their roots deep in the earth, their branches reaching toward the heavens. These trees held a primal power, a connection to the earth that no other beings possessed.

Gwydion would awaken this power, transforming the trees into living warriors, beings of wood and leaf, imbued with the strength of the earth and the wisdom of ages. They would march under his command, a formidable force against the darkness of Annwn.

But to do this, Gwydion needed to call upon the deepest magic, the oldest spells known only to those who understood the true language of nature. It was a magic that required not just words and gestures, but a deep communion with the spirits of the land, the very essence of the trees themselves.

With the weight of this task upon him, Gwydion journeyed into the heart of the forest, where the oldest and most powerful trees grew. The forest was a place of quiet majesty, where the air was thick with the scent of moss and the whisper of leaves. The trees here were ancient, their trunks wide and gnarled, their roots intertwined with the very fabric of the earth.

Gwydion stood among them, feeling the pulse of the forest around him. He knew that the trees were more than just plants; they were beings of wisdom, connected to the cycles of life and death, the rhythms of the earth. He reached out with his mind, speaking to the spirits of the trees, asking for their aid in the coming battle.

The trees, in their own way, responded. The air grew heavy with magic, and the ground seemed to hum with energy. Gwydion began to chant, his voice carrying the ancient words of power, a spell that would awaken the spirits of the trees and transform them into warriors.

The forest shivered as the spell took hold. The trees began to stir, their branches creaking, their roots pulling free from the earth. Slowly, the transformation began. The oak, the ash, the birch, the yew—all the trees of the forest began to reshape themselves, their trunks bending and twisting into forms resembling mighty warriors. Leaves rustled like the clink of armor, and the bark hardened into shields and weapons.

These tree-warriors were unlike any beings that had walked the earth before. They were imbued with the strength of the forest, their movements slow but powerful, their eyes glowing with the light of ancient wisdom. They were living embodiments of nature, called forth to fight for the balance of the world.

Gwydion, standing at the center of this transformation, felt the power of the forest flowing through him. He knew that the army he had summoned was ready to face the forces of Annwn. With a sense of both awe and determination, he prepared to lead them into battle, to reclaim the Cauldron of Inspiration and restore the harmony that had been disrupted.

The stage was set for the Battle of the Trees—a battle where the forces of nature would rise up against the darkness of the Otherworld, where the ancient spirits of the earth would fight to preserve the balance of the world.

With the army of tree-warriors standing tall and ready, Gwydion knew the time had come to lead them into the heart of Annwn, where Arawn waited with his dark forces. The air was thick with anticipation, the silence of the forest now replaced by the rustling of leaves and the creaking of ancient branches, as the living trees prepared for a battle unlike any the world had ever seen.

Gwydion stood at the forefront, his mind focused and sharp. He knew the way to Annwn, the secret paths that twisted through the fabric of reality, leading from the world of the living into the shadowy realm of the dead. With a wave of his hand, he opened a portal between the worlds, a shimmering gateway through which his army would march.

One by one, the tree-warriors stepped through the portal, their heavy footfalls echoing through the Otherworld as they entered the realm of Annwn. The land around them was dark and forbidding, shrouded in mist and shadow, the ground beneath their feet cold and unyielding. The air was thick with the scent of decay, and the sky above was an endless expanse of twilight, neither day nor night, a place caught between worlds.

Arawn had not been idle. The Lord of Annwn, sensing the intrusion into his domain, had gathered his own forces in preparation for the battle. His warriors were creatures of the Otherworld, beings of shadow and nightmare, their forms shifting and amorphous, their eyes glowing with a malevolent light. They were spirits of the dead, twisted and bound to Arawn's will, and they moved with an eerie grace, their bodies flickering like shadows in the dim light.

The two armies faced each other across a barren plain, the tree-warriors of Gwydion standing firm and resolute, their branches swaying gently in the cold breeze, while the dark forces of Annwn slithered and crawled, their movements unsettling and unnatural. The air between them crackled with energy, a tension that spoke of the power held by both sides.

Gwydion stepped forward, his voice carrying across the plain as he called out to Arawn. "Lord of Annwn, you have taken that which does not belong to you. Return the Cauldron of Inspiration, and we shall leave your realm in peace."

Arawn's voice echoed back, cold and unyielding, as if it came from the very stones of Annwn itself. "The cauldron is mine now, Gwydion. You will find no peace here, only the darkness of the Otherworld."

With those words, the battle began.

Arawn's forces surged forward, a wave of shadow and

darkness that swept across the plain like a storm. The creatures of Annwn attacked with a ferocity born of the underworld, their claws and teeth tearing at the tree-warriors with an unnatural strength. But the tree-warriors were not easily cowed. Their roots dug deep into the earth of Annwn, drawing strength from the very ground beneath them, their branches lashing out like whips, their bark as hard as iron.

The clash of the two armies was a sight to behold. The tree-warriors fought with a primal fury, their forms towering over the shadowy creatures of Annwn. The oak warriors were like living fortresses, their massive limbs crushing everything in their path, while the birch and ash moved with a swift, almost graceful precision, cutting down their enemies with deadly accuracy. The yews, dark and ancient, seemed to absorb the shadows around them, their very presence a challenge to the darkness of Annwn.

Gwydion, in the midst of the battle, wielded his magic with precision and power. He called down lightning from the sky, the bolts striking the ground with a deafening roar, scattering Arawn's forces and lighting up the plain with flashes of blinding light. He wove spells of protection around his warriors, their forms shimmering with a magical barrier that repelled the attacks of the Otherworldly creatures.

But Arawn was not to be outdone. The Lord of Annwn commanded the shadows themselves, his forces moving with a speed and agility that seemed impossible. He unleashed a swarm of spirits, their wails piercing the air, disorienting the tree-warriors and driving them back. He summoned the cold wind of the underworld, a gale that howled across the plain, freezing the air and sapping the strength of Gwydion's forces.

The battle raged on, neither side willing to give ground. The tree-warriors, though powerful and resilient, were beginning to tire, their movements slowing as the relentless assault of

Arawn's forces took its toll. The creatures of Annwn, tireless and driven by their master's will, continued to press the attack, their numbers seemingly endless.

Gwydion, seeing the tide of battle turning against him, knew he had to act quickly. He called upon the deepest reserves of his magic, drawing on the ancient power of the earth and the sky, the forces of nature that had shaped the world since time began. With a shout, he unleashed a spell of transformation, a wave of energy that rippled through the battlefield.

The tree-warriors responded to Gwydion's call, their forms shifting and changing once again. Where once they had been warriors of wood and leaf, now they became something more. The oaks became giants, their forms swelling to twice their size, their limbs thickening into massive clubs that smashed through the ranks of Arawn's forces. The birches and ash grew wings of leaves, taking to the sky and diving down upon their enemies with the speed of falcons. The yews, dark and mysterious, seemed to melt into the shadows, reappearing behind the enemy lines, striking with deadly precision before fading back into the darkness.

The tide of battle began to turn. The creatures of Annwn, for all their power, could not withstand the onslaught of the transformed tree-warriors. The plain was filled with the sounds of battle, the clash of wood against shadow, the cries of the fallen, the roar of Gwydion's magic.

Arawn, seeing his forces falter, called upon the deepest magic of Annwn, summoning a darkness that blotted out the sky, a void that seemed to consume all light and hope. But Gwydion was ready. With a final, powerful incantation, he called down a beam of pure light, a lance of energy that pierced the darkness and struck Arawn's forces with a blinding intensity.

The creatures of Annwn, unable to withstand the light, fell back, their forms dissolving into shadows that were swept away by the wind. The tree-warriors, bathed in the glow of Gwydion's magic, pressed forward, driving the remaining forces of Annwn before them.

Finally, with a great shout, Gwydion's army broke through the last of Arawn's defenses, reaching the heart of Annwn where the Cauldron of Inspiration was kept. Arawn, defeated, withdrew into the depths of his realm, his dark presence retreating before the light of Gwydion's victory.

The battle was won.

The tree-warriors, their purpose fulfilled, began to return to their original forms. The oak giants shrank back to their normal size, their limbs becoming branches once more. The birches and ash, their wings folding back into their trunks, settled down upon the earth. The yews, their shadowy forms solidifying, stood tall and still, their bark dark and impenetrable.

Gwydion, exhausted but triumphant, approached the Cauldron of Inspiration. The cauldron glowed with a soft, ethereal light, the Awen flowing within it like liquid silver. He knew that the balance had been restored, the cauldron returned to its rightful place.

With the cauldron in hand, Gwydion led his army of trees back through the portal to the world of the living. The battle of Annwn was over, the forces of darkness defeated, and the cauldron reclaimed.

As the portal closed behind them, the tree-warriors returned to the forests from which they had come, their forms once again merging with the earth, their roots digging deep into the soil. The forest was quiet once more, the battle a memory that would live on in the hearts of those who had witnessed it.

Folk Tales from Ireland

Upon reaching the heart of the forest, Gwydion found a sacred grove, a place where the earth's energy was at its strongest. It was here that he decided to return the cauldron, placing it carefully upon a stone altar that stood in the center of the grove. The cauldron's light seemed to blend with the sunlight filtering through the trees, casting a golden glow across the clearing.

Gwydion spoke a few words of thanks, his voice carrying through the grove like a gentle breeze. He knew that the cauldron was safe here, in the care of the forest and the earth, where its power would be protected and its influence would continue to inspire those who sought wisdom and creativity.

With the cauldron safely returned, Gwydion felt a sense of completion. The battle had been fought, the cauldron reclaimed, and the balance restored. But he also knew that the story of the Battle of the Trees would live on, a tale that would be told by bards and druids, passed down through the generations as a reminder of the power of nature and the magic that flows through the world.

As he left the grove, Gwydion could feel the eyes of the forest upon him, a silent blessing from the ancient trees that had fought beside him. He walked with a renewed sense of purpose, knowing that the natural world was a force to be respected and revered, a force that could rise up in times of need to protect the balance of life.

Gwydion, his task complete, knew that the story of the Battle of the Trees would be told for generations to come, a tale of magic, courage, and the enduring power of nature.

F.T. Weaver

Cultural Significance and Other Cultural Facts About "The Battle of the Trees (Cad Goddeu)"

"The Battle of the Trees" (Cad Goddeu) is a mystical and enigmatic poem found in the Book of Taliesin, one of the most important medieval Welsh manuscripts. The poem is part of Welsh mythology, a rich tapestry of legends and folklore that forms the backbone of Celtic cultural heritage. "The Battle of the Trees" is not just a tale of a fantastical battle; it is a deeply symbolic narrative that intertwines themes of nature, magic, and the power of words and knowledge. Its cultural significance is profound, influencing not just the mythology and literature of Wales but also the broader Celtic traditions.

The Poetic and Symbolic Nature of "Cad Goddeu"

"Cad Goddeu" is a poem that is steeped in symbolism and allegory, making it one of the most complex and intriguing pieces of Welsh mythology. Unlike more straightforward heroic narratives, this poem resists easy interpretation, inviting readers to explore its layers of meaning. It is a text that operates on multiple levels, blending mythological storytelling with deep philosophical and spiritual insights.

The central event of the poem is a battle where trees and plants are magically transformed into warriors. This transformation is performed by the magician Gwydion, a central figure in Welsh mythology who embodies the power of magic, wisdom, and cunning. The poem's focus on nature as both a setting and a participant in the battle underscores the deep connection between the natural world and the spiritual or magical realms in Celtic thought.

In Celtic culture, trees were seen as sacred beings, embodying the spirits of the earth and serving as connections between the heavens, the earth, and the underworld. The transformation of trees into warriors in "Cad Goddeu" can be seen as an expression of the animistic belief that all elements of nature are alive and possess their own spiritual essence. This belief is reflected in the poem's rich imagery and its invocation of various trees and plants, each with its own symbolic meaning.

For example, the oak is often associated with strength and endurance, the birch with renewal and purification, and the yew with death and rebirth. The poem's use of these trees as warriors suggests that the battle is not just a physical conflict but a metaphysical struggle involving the fundamental forces of life, death, and transformation.

The Role of Gwydion and the Power of Magic

Gwydion is a central figure in Welsh mythology, known for his magical abilities and his role as a trickster and a sage. In "Cad Goddeu," Gwydion's transformation of trees into warriors demonstrates the power of magic in Celtic mythology. Magic in this context is not merely about supernatural feats; it is about the mastery of knowledge, the ability to manipulate the world through words, and the deep understanding of the natural world.

Gwydion's magic is closely tied to the concept of Awen, the divine inspiration that flows through poets, bards, and druids in Celtic culture. Awen is seen as a sacred force, the source of creativity, wisdom, and poetic insight. In the poem, the act of bringing the trees to life is an act of creative magic, a manifestation of Awen that transforms the natural world into an active participant in the cosmic struggle.

The poem also emphasizes the power of words and knowledge. Gwydion's ability to name the trees and invoke their spirits is what gives him the power to transform them. In Celtic tradition, names are powerful, and the act of naming something is an act of creation and control. This ties into the broader theme of the power of language in Celtic culture, where poets and bards were highly revered for their ability to shape reality through their words.

The Battle as a Metaphor

The battle in "Cad Goddeu" is not a typical martial conflict but rather a symbolic struggle that can be interpreted on several levels. On one level, it represents the eternal conflict between light and darkness, life and death, order and chaos. The forces of nature, personified by the trees, are pitted against the forces of the Otherworld, represented by Arawn, the Lord of Annwn. This battle is a microcosm of the larger cosmic struggle that defines much of Celtic mythology.

On another level, the battle can be seen as a metaphor for the internal struggle of the soul or the intellect. The trees, with their deep roots and towering forms, symbolize the different aspects of the self—strength, wisdom, flexibility, and endurance. The battle could be interpreted as an internal conflict where these qualities are mobilized to overcome the forces of darkness or ignorance.

The Cauldron of Inspiration, which is the object of the conflict, further deepens the symbolic nature of the battle. The cauldron is a powerful symbol in Celtic mythology, often representing the source of knowledge, rebirth, and transformation. In "Cad Goddeu," the cauldron's theft by Arawn represents the disruption of the natural order and the loss of divine inspiration. The battle to reclaim the cauldron is thus a struggle to restore balance and ensure the continuation of the flow of Awen.

The Place of "Cad Goddeu" in Welsh Mythology

"Cad Goddeu" occupies a unique place in Welsh mythology due to its enigmatic nature and its deep symbolic content. It is part of the Book of Taliesin, a manuscript that contains some of the earliest and most important examples of Welsh poetry. The poem's association with Taliesin, a legendary bard and a figure of immense wisdom and mystical insight, further enhances its cultural significance.

The Book of Taliesin itself is a cornerstone of Welsh literary tradition, and "Cad Goddeu" is one of its most studied and debated pieces. The poem reflects the rich oral tradition of the Celts, where stories and knowledge were passed down through generations of bards and druids. These tales were not just entertainment; they were a means of preserving and transmitting cultural values, spiritual beliefs, and the collective wisdom of the people.

The poem's focus on the natural world and its deep connection to the cycles of life, death, and rebirth is reflective of the Celtic worldview, which saw the natural and supernatural worlds as intimately intertwined. The Celts believed that the land itself was alive, inhabited by spirits and gods who could influence human affairs. "Cad Goddeu" encapsulates this belief, portraying the trees not just as passive elements of the landscape but as active, powerful beings capable of influencing the outcome of cosmic events.

Influence and Legacy

The influence of "Cad Goddeu" extends beyond its original cultural context, resonating in various forms of art, literature, and modern pagan practices. The poem's themes of transformation, the power of nature, and the interplay between light and dark have inspired countless interpretations and adaptations over the centuries.

In modern times, "Cad Goddeu" has been embraced by the neo-pagan and druidic movements, which see the poem as a celebration of the natural world and its sacredness. The poem's portrayal of trees as sentient beings with their own agency and power aligns with contemporary environmentalism and the belief in the interconnectedness of all life.

The story also continues to be a source of inspiration for writers, poets, and artists who are drawn to its mystical and enigmatic nature. Its imagery of trees coming to life, its portrayal of a magical battle, and its deep philosophical underpinnings provide a rich tapestry for creative exploration.

Interpretation Challenges and Scholarly Debate

The interpretation of "Cad Goddeu" has been a subject of scholarly debate for many years. The poem's dense symbolism, its fragmented narrative, and its archaic language make it a challenging text to fully understand. Some scholars see it as an allegory for the initiation rites of the druids, where the transformation of the trees represents the awakening of spiritual insight. Others interpret it as a cosmological myth, where the battle symbolizes the cycles of nature and the eternal struggle between opposing forces.

The poem's connection to Taliesin, both as a historical figure and a legendary bard, adds another layer of complexity. Taliesin is often seen as a bridge between the mortal and divine realms, and his association with the poem suggests that "Cad Goddeu" is more than just a myth; it is a meditation on the nature of knowledge, creativity, and the divine.

The varying interpretations of "Cad Goddeu" reflect the richness of Celtic mythology and its capacity to convey multiple meanings through a single narrative. The poem's ambiguity and its open-ended nature allow for a wide range of interpretations, *each adding to the depth and mystery of the tale.*

Conclusion

"The Battle of the Trees" (Cad Goddeu) is a powerful and enduring piece of Welsh mythology that encapsulates the richness of Celtic cultural and spiritual traditions. Its themes of nature, magic, and transformation are woven into a narrative that is both enigmatic and profound. The poem serves as a testament to the Celtic belief in the sacredness of the natural world and the power of words and knowledge to shape reality.

Its cultural significance lies not only in its literary and symbolic content but also in its influence on later traditions and its continuing relevance in contemporary interpretations of Celtic spirituality. "Cad Goddeu" remains a central part of the Welsh mythological canon, a poem that invites readers and scholars alike to delve into its mysteries and uncover the layers of meaning that have made it a timeless piece of cultural heritage.

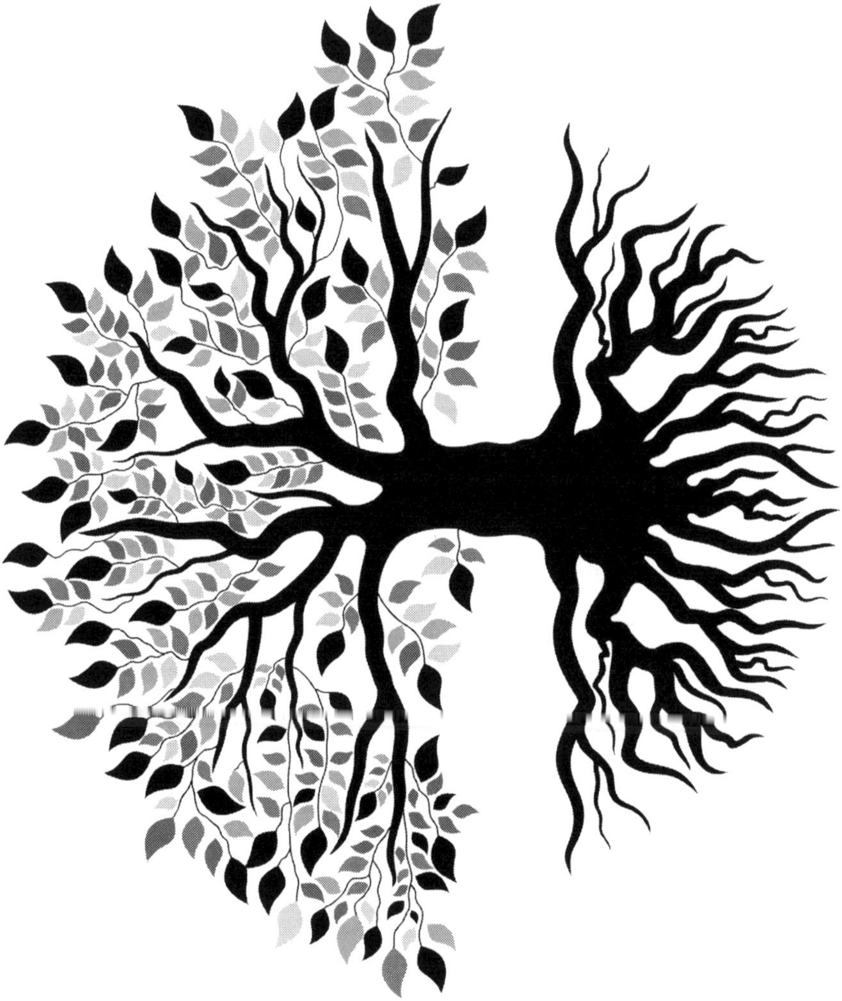

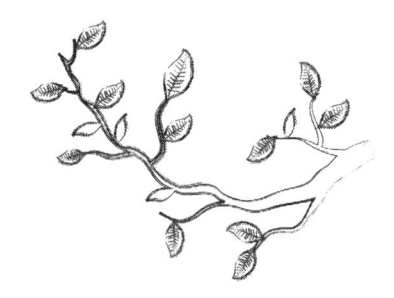

The Tale of The Wooing of Étaín

In the mystical realms of ancient Ireland, where the Tuatha Dé Danann ruled over the land with their otherworldly powers, there lived a noble being named Midir. Midir was one of the most esteemed members of the Tuatha Dé Danann, known for his wisdom, charm, and the beauty of his realm in Brí Léith. Midir's life was one of luxury and power, but it was also marked by a deep and passionate love for a woman of extraordinary beauty, Étaín.

Étaín was not originally of the Tuatha Dé Danann but was born among them, a woman whose radiance and grace captured the hearts of all who beheld her. Her beauty was such that the very sun seemed to shine more brightly when she walked under its rays, and the winds sang in delight when they touched her hair. Midir fell deeply in love with Étaín, and she became the center of his world, his companion and his joy.

However, Midir's love for Étaín was not without complications. Midir already had a wife, Fuamnach, a woman of great power and formidable magic. Fuamnach was jealous of Étaín's beauty and the love that Midir lavished upon her.

Her heart burned with envy, and she could not bear the thought of being displaced in Midir's affections.

Fuamnach's jealousy drove her to commit a series of cruel acts against Étaín. Using her powerful magic, she transformed Étaín into a pool of water, then into a worm, and finally into a beautiful purple butterfly. In this delicate form, Étaín was blown by the winds across the lands, a helpless creature caught in the currents of fate.

Despite her transformation, Étaín's beauty and grace were not diminished. As a butterfly, she was carried by the breeze until she found refuge in the palace of Aengus Óg, the god of love and youth, who recognized her true nature. Aengus protected Étaín, creating a magical bower for her to live in, where she was safe from the dangers of the world.

But even Aengus could not protect Étaín from the full extent of Fuamnach's wrath. Fuamnach continued to seek out Étaín, and when she discovered that Étaín was under Aengus's protection, she unleashed a fierce wind that drove the butterfly from Aengus's palace and out into the world once more. Étaín was blown across the seas and lands for seven long years, a wandering soul in a fragile form, until finally, she was carried into the cup of a woman who was drinking from a vessel of water.

The woman who drank from the cup was the wife of Étar, a chieftain of the Ulaid, and through this mystical means, Étaín was reborn into the mortal world as a human child. She grew up in the household of Étar, unaware of her true origins but retaining the same beauty and grace that had once captivated the hearts of the Tuatha Dé Danann.

As she grew, Étaín's beauty became the talk of the land, and her fame spread far and wide. Men from all corners of Ireland came to seek her hand in marriage, but it was Eochu Airem, the High King of Ireland, who won her love and took her

Folk Tales from Ireland

as his queen. Eochu was a wise and just king, and under his rule, Ireland prospered. He was deeply in love with Étaín, and she brought light and joy to his court.

Yet, despite her happiness, Étaín's past was not entirely forgotten. The memory of her life among the Tuatha Dé Danann lingered in the depths of her soul, like a distant dream that could not be fully remembered. She lived as a mortal queen, beloved by her husband and people, but the threads of fate had not finished weaving her story.

In the otherworldly realm of Brí Léith, Midir had never ceased to love Étaín. His heart ached for the loss of his beloved, and he longed to be reunited with her. Though he knew that she had been reborn as a mortal, he was determined to find her and bring her back to his side.

The tale of Étaín's rebirth and Midir's enduring love for her sets the stage for one of the most beautiful and tragic stories in Irish mythology. It is a tale that weaves together themes of love, jealousy, transformation, and the enduring power of the bonds that connect us across time and space.

As Midir begins his search for Étaín, the story will unfold with all the richness and depth of an ancient myth, leading to a series of events that will test the limits of love and loyalty, and ultimately decide the fate of Étaín, Midir, and those who are drawn into their story.

The years passed in the mortal world, and Étaín, now the beloved queen of King Eochu Airem, lived a life of quiet contentment, unaware of her true origins. The court of Eochu was a place of splendor and peace, and Étaín's beauty was celebrated by all who beheld her. Yet, within the otherworldly realm of the Tuatha Dé Danann, Midir's heart remained heavy with longing for his lost love.

Midir had never forgotten Étaín. Despite the passage of time and the changes wrought by her rebirth into the mortal world, his love for her burned as fiercely as ever. He could not rest until he had found her and brought her back to Brí Léith. Midir's quest for Étaín became an obsession, driving him to search every corner of the earth and beyond.

Through his magical powers, Midir eventually discovered Étaín's fate—that she had been reborn as a mortal woman, living in the court of Eochu Airem, the High King of Ireland. Determined to win her back, Midir devised a plan to approach Eochu's court and seek an audience with the king. He knew that he could not simply take Étaín from her husband; he would need to win her back through more subtle means.

Midir arrived at the court of Eochu in the guise of a noble stranger, his true identity hidden by enchantment. He was welcomed as a guest, for Eochu was known for his hospitality and generosity. Midir's charm and wisdom quickly won him favor in the court, and he became a trusted companion of the king.

One day, as Midir and Eochu sat together, enjoying a game of fidchell, an ancient board game of strategy and skill, Midir proposed a wager. He suggested that if he won the game, Eochu would grant him a boon of his choosing. Eochu, confident in his own abilities and intrigued by the challenge, agreed to the wager without hesitation.

The game commenced, and as they played, Midir used his magical prowess to subtly influence the outcome. Despite Eochu's best efforts, Midir won the game. When Eochu asked what boon Midir desired, Midir smiled and replied, "I ask for nothing more than to embrace your queen, Étaín, before your court."

Eochu, taken aback by the request, was both puzzled and concerned. He had promised to grant Midir a boon, but he was wary of allowing another man to come so close to his beloved wife. Yet, bound by his word, he reluctantly agreed, setting a date for the fulfillment of the promise.

On the appointed day, Midir appeared in Eochu's court, dressed in finery and exuding an otherworldly presence that captivated all who saw him. The court gathered to witness the event, curious about this mysterious stranger and the unusual request he had made.

When Étaín entered the hall, her beauty was as radiant as ever, and Midir's heart ached with the intensity of his love for her. As she approached, Midir took her gently by the hand and, in the sight of all, drew her close and embraced her. In that moment, something stirred within Étaín's soul—a flicker of recognition, as if a long-forgotten dream had come to life.

Midir, sensing the connection, whispered words of love and remembrance into Étaín's ear. He spoke of Brí Léith, of their life together before her transformation, and of the love that had bound them across time and space. Étaín listened, her heart moved by the depth of his emotion, and though she did not fully understand, she felt a powerful pull towards this stranger who seemed to know her so intimately.

Seeing the reaction of his queen, Eochu grew uneasy. He realized that there was more to this encounter than he had anticipated. He suspected that Midir was not an ordinary man, but someone with otherworldly power and a deeper connection to Étaín than he had first thought.

Midir, sensing Eochu's discomfort, released Étaín and spoke to the king. "I have fulfilled the terms of our wager, and now I must ask you to honor my request. Allow me to take Étaín with me, as she was once mine before she was yours."

Eochu, shocked by the audacity of the request, refused. "Étaín is my wife and queen, and I will not part with her. You have made a bold request, but I cannot grant it."

Midir, undeterred, proposed another challenge. "If you refuse to let her go, then let us play one more game of fidchell.

If I win, you will grant me Étaín without further dispute. If you win, I will leave your court and trouble you no more."

Eochu, though wary, could not resist the challenge, for he was a man of pride and confidence in his skills. He agreed to the terms, and the game began.

This time, the stakes were even higher, and the tension in the room was palpable. The court watched in silence as the two men played, their moves calculated and deliberate. Midir, with his magical influence, again turned the game in his favor, and once more, he emerged victorious.

Eochu, bound by the terms of the wager, was forced to honor his promise. Yet, he was not willing to let Étaín go so easily. He declared that Midir could return for Étaín in one month's time, during which Eochu planned to fortify his court and prepare for any attempt Midir might make to take her by force.

Midir accepted the terms and left the court, but he had no intention of waiting passively. He began to prepare for the moment when he would reclaim Étaín, calling upon the full extent of his magical powers.

When the appointed day arrived, Midir returned to Eochu's court, this time accompanied by a swirling mist that filled the hall. The air crackled with the energy of his magic, and the court was gripped by an eerie silence.

Midir appeared before Étaín and Eochu, his presence commanding and undeniable. He extended his hand to Étaín, and as she took it, the mist enveloped them both. Before the eyes of the stunned court, they rose into the air, transformed into swans, and flew out of the hall and into the sky, their forms shining with a radiant light.

Eochu, realizing that he had been outwitted, was filled with rage and despair. He gathered his warriors and set out in pursuit, determined to retrieve his queen. But Midir and Étaín had returned to the otherworldly realm of Brí Léith, a place beyond the reach of mortal men.

In Brí Léith, Midir and Étaín were reunited, their love stronger than ever, having transcended the boundaries of time, space, and even mortality.

Cultural Significance and Other Cultural Facts About "The Wooing of Étaín"

"The Wooing of Étaín" (Tochmarc Étaíne) is one of the most intricate and beautiful tales from the Mythological Cycle of Irish mythology. This tale, rich in symbolic meaning and cultural resonance, encapsulates many of the core themes of Irish myth, including love, transformation, and the interaction between the mortal and otherworldly realms. It is a story that has captivated audiences for centuries and continues to be a key part of Ireland's cultural and literary heritage.

The Mythological Cycle and Its Place in Irish Culture

The Mythological Cycle is one of the four major cycles of Irish mythology, alongside the Ulster Cycle, the Fenian Cycle, and the Historical Cycle. It primarily deals with the ancient gods and goddesses of Ireland, particularly the Tuatha Dé Danann, a race of supernatural beings who ruled Ireland before the arrival of the Milesians, the ancestors of the Irish people.

"The Wooing of Étaín" is central to the Mythological Cycle, intertwining the lives of mortals and the Tuatha Dé Danann in a tale that explores the complexities of love, power, and destiny. The story reflects the deep-seated belief in Ireland that the boundaries between the human and the divine, the natural and the supernatural, are fluid and often crossed.

Themes of Love and Transformation

At its heart, "The Wooing of Étaín" is a love story, but it is one that transcends the ordinary and delves into the extraordinary. The love between Midir and Étaín is not just a romantic bond but a connection that endures through time, space, and even across different lifetimes. This idea of love as an eternal and unbreakable force is a common theme in Celtic mythology, where the bonds between souls are seen as lasting beyond death and the physical world.

The story also explores the theme of transformation, both literal and metaphorical. Étaín's various transformations—from a beautiful woman to a butterfly, and back to a mortal woman—symbolize the fluidity of identity and the cyclical nature of life and existence. Transformation is a recurring motif in Irish mythology, often representing the idea that change is a fundamental part of the universe, and that nothing, not even identity, is fixed.

The transformations Étaín undergoes can also be seen as a reflection of the natural world's cycles—birth, death, and rebirth—echoing the seasons and the agricultural cycles that were so important in ancient Ireland. The story suggests that just as the earth renews itself, so too can love and identity be renewed, even after great trials and suffering.

The Interplay Between the Mortal and Otherworldly Realms

One of the most significant aspects of "The Wooing of Étaín" is its depiction of the interaction between the mortal world and the Otherworld, the realm of the Tuatha Dé Danann. In Irish mythology, the Otherworld is a parallel dimension that is often depicted as a place of eternal youth, beauty, and magic, but also *of danger and unpredictability. It is a world that is always close to the mortal realm, with portals and pathways that can be crossed under certain conditions or by certain individuals.*

Étaín's movement between these worlds—her life among the Tuatha Dé Danann, her rebirth as a mortal, and her eventual return to the Otherworld with Midir—illustrates the permeability of these boundaries. The story reflects the belief that the gods and other supernatural beings are not distant or disconnected from human life, but are deeply involved in it, influencing events and relationships.

This interplay between worlds also underscores the idea that life is full of hidden layers and that what we perceive as reality is just one aspect of a much larger, more complex universe. The fluidity between the mortal and the divine realms in "The Wooing of Étaín" is a reminder of the mysteries that lie beneath the surface of everyday life, a common theme in Celtic mythology.

The Role of Fate and Free Will

"The Wooing of Étaín" also explores the tension between fate and free will, a theme that is prevalent in many mythological traditions. The characters in the story are often guided by forces beyond their control—prophecies, magical transformations, and the interventions of the gods—but they also exercise their own agency, making choices that shape their destinies.

Étaín, in particular, is a character caught between these forces. She is transformed and manipulated by the jealousy of Fuamnach, yet she retains her own sense of identity and agency. Her decision to return with Midir, even after being reunited with her mortal husband Eochu, suggests a deep recognition of her true self and her eternal bond with Midir. This choice can be seen as an assertion of free will in the face of overwhelming circumstances, a theme that resonates with the idea of personal autonomy in the face of destiny.

Midir's persistence in seeking out Étaín, despite the obstacles placed in his way, also reflects the importance of free will and determination. His willingness to challenge Eochu and to invoke the laws of the Otherworld to win back Étaín underscores the belief that while fate may set certain paths, the choices individuals make are crucial in determining their outcomes.

The Cultural Impact of the Story

"The Wooing of Étaín" has had a profound impact on Irish literature and culture, influencing both ancient and modern works. The story has been retold and adapted numerous times, each retelling adding new layers of interpretation and meaning. Its themes of love, loss, and reunion resonate deeply with Irish cultural values, particularly the importance of loyalty, the sanctity of marriage, and the enduring nature of true love.

In literature, the story has inspired poets and writers, including W.B. Yeats, who often drew on Irish mythological themes in his work. Yeats was fascinated by the idea of the Otherworld and the interaction between the mortal and divine, themes that are central to "The Wooing of Étaín". The story's emphasis on transformation and the cyclical nature of existence also aligns with Yeats's own mystical beliefs.

The tale's influence extends beyond literature into the realms of music, art, and performance. It has inspired traditional Irish music, with ballads and songs that recount the tale of Étaín and Midir's love and the trials they endure. Visual artists have also been drawn to the story, depicting scenes of Étaín's beauty, her transformations, and the magical landscapes of the Otherworld.

In modern Irish culture, "The Wooing of Étaín" continues to be a touchstone for discussions of identity, heritage, and the connection to the past. The story is often taught in schools and is a key part of the cultural education that connects contemporary Irish people to their mythological roots. It serves as a reminder of the richness of Irish mythology and the ways in which these ancient stories still hold relevance today.

The Symbolism of Étaín

Étaín herself is a deeply symbolic figure, representing beauty, grace, and the idea of the eternal feminine. Her multiple lives and transformations can be seen as a metaphor for the resilience of the human spirit and the enduring power of love. Despite the hardships and transformations she endures, Étaín remains a figure of dignity and strength, embodying the idea that true beauty and love are eternal and unchanging, even as the world around them shifts.

Étaín's connection to water—first as a transformed pool of water and later as a butterfly carried by the wind—ties her to the natural elements, symbolizing the fluidity of life and the constant flow of time. Water in Celtic symbolism is often associated with rebirth and transformation, further emphasizing these themes in her story.

Her relationship with Midir, and the obstacles they face, also highlights the idea of love as a force that transcends not only time but also the physical and metaphysical boundaries that separate individuals. Their love is portrayed as both deeply personal and universally significant, reflecting the belief that love is a fundamental force that shapes both the human and divine worlds.

Conclusion

"The Wooing of Étaín" is a story that encapsulates the richness of Irish mythology, blending themes of love, *transformation, and the interplay between the mortal and divine. Its cultural significance lies in its ability to convey complex ideas about identity, fate, and the nature of reality through a narrative that is both enchanting and profound.*

The tale's enduring appeal is a testament to the power of storytelling in Irish culture, where myths and legends are not just remnants of the past but living traditions that continue to inform and inspire. "The Wooing of Étaín" remains a vital part of Ireland's cultural heritage, a story that speaks to the universal experiences of love, loss, and the search for meaning in a world that is both mysterious and ever-changing.

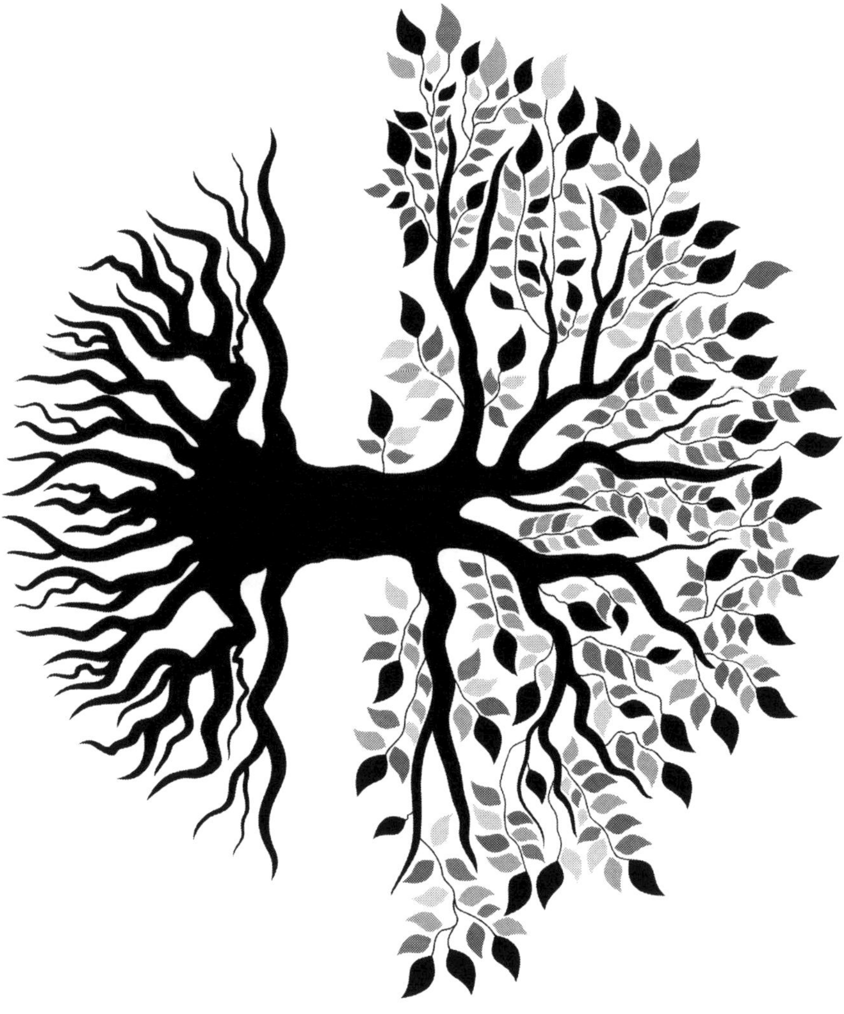

F.T. Weaver

Epilogue

As the final pages of this collection close, you are left with the lingering echoes of Ireland's ancient legends—tales of love, loss, bravery, and magic that have been passed down through the centuries, surviving the tides of time and change.

These stories, though rooted in a distant past, are far from forgotten. They live on in the whispered winds that sweep across the green hills, in the gentle lapping of waves against the rugged coastlines, and in the hearts of those who cherish the rich tapestry of Ireland's cultural heritage.

The myths and legends within this book are more than just tales; they are the soul of a people, a connection to the land, and a bridge between the seen and unseen worlds. Through the exploits of heroes like Cú Chulainn, the tragic fate of Deirdre, and the magical transformations of Étaín, we glimpse a world where the boundaries between the human and the divine blur, and where every shadow holds the promise of the extraordinary.

In these stories, there is a reminder of the power of storytelling itself. They show us how stories can preserve history, impart wisdom, and evoke emotions that transcend time and place. The lessons and themes woven into these tales—of courage, sacrifice, the inevitable pull of destiny, and the enduring *nature of love—resonate as strongly today as they did in the days when these legends were first told around the flickering flames of a hearth.*

As you set this book aside, may you carry with you a piece of that ancient magic, a spark of the wonder that has been ignited by these timeless stories. Whether you are returning to the world of everyday life or still wandering through the misty realms of myth and magic, remember that these legends are never far away. They are always waiting to be rediscovered, to be retold, and to be lived again in the imaginations of those who dare to dream.

The land of Ireland, with its rugged beauty and deep mystery, will continue to be a source of inspiration for generations to come. And these tales, passed down from one storyteller to the next, will remain a testament to the enduring power of myth and the unbreakable bond between a people and their stories.

May the enchantment of these legends stay with you, and may you find your own path through the stories yet to be told. The journey doesn't end here—this is just the beginning of your own exploration of the rich and boundless world of Irish folklore.

Until we meet again in the pages of another tale, may the road rise up to meet you, and may the wind be always at your back.

THE END

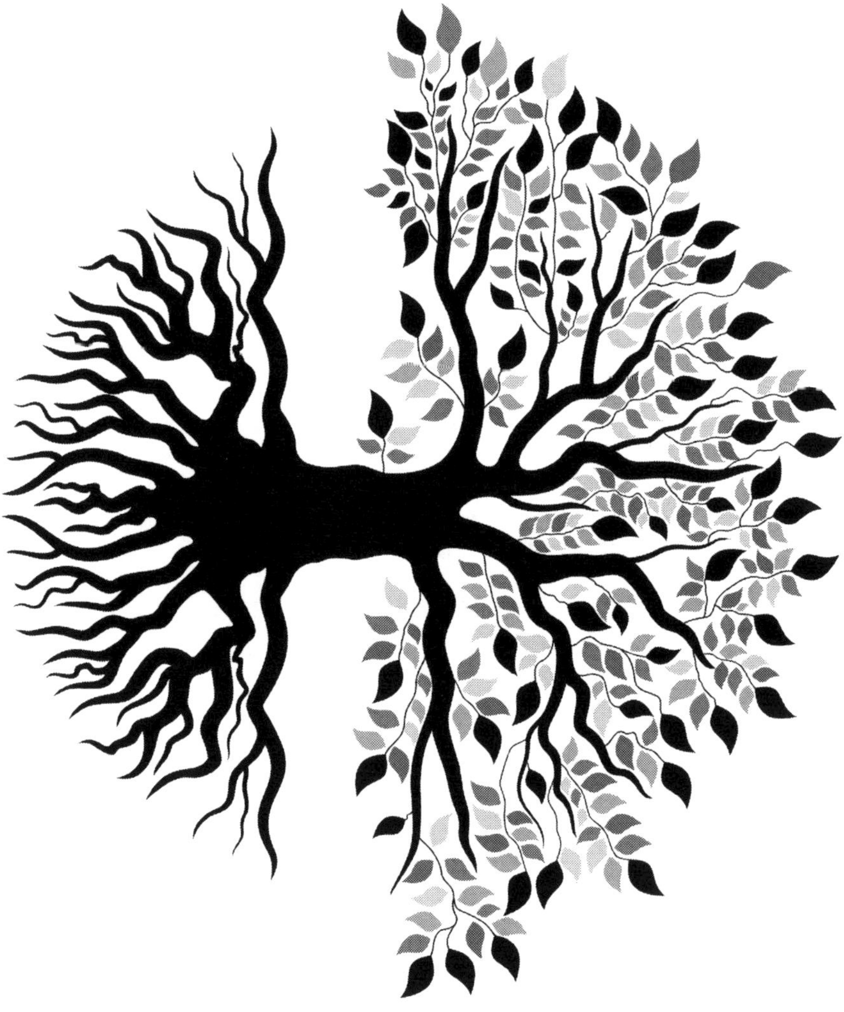

Join Our Enchanted Community!

Loved these timeless tales of magic and wonder? The adventure doesn't have to end here! Join our enchanted community and stay connected with a world of folklore, fairy tales, and much more.

By signing up for our mailing list, you'll receive:

Exclusive Updates: Be the first to know about upcoming releases, special editions, and new collections of folk tales from around the world.

Behind-the-Scenes Content: Discover the fascinating history and cultural insights behind your favorite stories.

Special Offers: Enjoy exclusive discounts, giveaways, and promotions available only to our subscribers.

Bonus Stories: Receive additional tales and magical content delivered straight to your inbox.

Don't miss out on the magic! **Scan the QR code below** to join our mailing list and embark on even more adventures.

Keep the stories alive, share the enchantment, and let the journey continue!

With Warmest wishes,
The Folk Tales Team

Printed in Great Britain
by Amazon

e1d83738-741a-44f5-ab4a-4ab60fbd7ba3R01